Speech Handbook

Speech Handbook

Speech Handbook

by

Harry Grinnell Barnes

SECOND EDITION

PRENTICE-HALL, INC.

Englewood Cliffs, N. J.

PRENTICE-HALL SPEECH SERIES

LIBRARY OF CONGRESS CATALOG CARD NUMBER: 59–7719

Current printing (last digit):
16   15   14   13   12   11   10   9   8   7

PRINTED IN THE UNITED STATES OF AMERICA
83162—C

Preface

Dr. Barnes first wrote the *Speech Handbook* to be used in the required course in *Principles of Speech* at the State University of Iowa. That was more than 20 years ago. Thousands of copies of the first edition have been used since then in college classes, high school classes, and programs in adult education.

In 1951 Dr. Barnes and the publisher agreed on a plan of revision and much of the work had been done at the time of his death. Early in 1957 the publisher honored me by asking me to complete the revision. I was happy to accept because I taught under Dr. Barnes at Iowa, and I have used the *Speech Handbook* many times since.

The first edition was built on the concept that the speech needs and abilities of students should determine the matter of a speech course. There were diagnostic materials, explanations of the fundamental processes of speech and the basic attributes of effective speaking, speaking assignments, word lists for pronunciation and articulation drill, and forms for the measurement of student achievement in speech making and reading aloud. Dr. Barnes planned to include most of these same features in the revision, with some changes in format and wording. He also planned to include a new section on the skills of reading aloud, together with some materials to be used for extemporaneous reading.

PREFACE

Wherever his words for this revision existed, I have kept them. Where only notes existed, I have done my best to write what I think he would have accepted.

In the first edition of this book, Dr. Barnes acknowledged his appreciation for contributing to his insight into the nature, function, and teaching of speech to J. P. Ryan, Edward C. Mabie, Lee Edward Travis, Raymond H. Wheeler, and Charles H. Woolbert.

In 1953 he wrote a dedication page for the new edition, inscribing it to "Ensign Harry Grinnell Barnes, Jr., United States Naval Academy, 'Who Won The Prize.'"

The editor wishes to acknowledge the kindness of the Harold Ober Associates, New York, for permission to print portions of *That Pup* by Ellis Parker Butler, and to Miss Erick Berry for permission to print portions of her story *Sojo*.

DON STREETER
Chairman, Department of Speech
The University of Houston

Speech Handbook

PART ONE

Your Speech Inventory

1   **A speech inventory—why?**

One of the wise practises of modern educational methods is to begin a course "from where the students are now." We may not like where they are. We may wish they were much more able than they are. We may even think they will never do the work of the course. Whatever we think, we should begin, with that particular class, from where they are now.

And so it is with this course. We need to take inventory of your needs and abilities. We want to know where you are now in your progress in speaking effectively.

Experienced teachers will pretty well know "where you are now." They know about how much experience a class like yours has had and about what the inventory will show. But *you* need to know something about it, too. Therefore, we find out where you stand and go on from there. The assignments in this book are built on the inventories of many hundreds of students. It is likely that yours will show many of the same strengths and weaknesses that the others have shown. But we need to find out again, from *you*. We need to know *you*.

Remember *you*, the speaker, are not exactly like any other speaker in any other class. As you participate in the work of this class you will get to know your classmates better than you will in nearly any other course, and they will come to know you equally well. It is you as a person that we get to know. That is the justification for thinking that a course in public speaking is, in a way, a course in "personality development."

2 What does this inventory include?

This inventory includes many of the things that we believe are important to know in order to help you get the most benefit from this course. These things include a little about your personal background and examples of your speaking and reading aloud. There are six steps in this inventory: (1) your background; (2) the basic processes; (3) the essential skills of speech making; (4) the essential skills of reading aloud; (5) phonation; and (6) articulation.

Your background. It makes a difference who you are. Some people have a background that may already have helped them become better speakers than others may ever become. Some may have a background that has hindered their making progress in speech making. You and your instructor should understand the parts of your background that might help you become a better speaker.

Please turn to the inventory assignments in Section 29.

The basic processes of speech. When you speak, under any circumstances, whether in public or in private conversation, you create ideas, formulating them through the use of words into thought units (usually sentences), and you express them through the activity of the nerves and muscles of your body. This action results in vocal tones, speech sounds, and bodily movements. For convenience of study, these processes are classified as follows:

Adjustment to the speaking situation. This process involves the management of the functioning of your entire bodily mechanism during speech. Speakers who are not well adjusted to the speaking situation may be ill at ease, unnatural, tense, nervous, hesitant, uncertain, or unable to speak coherently. The well-adjusted speaker, on the other hand, is likely to be poised, natural, calm, speaking directly to his listeners.

Formulation of thought. Single words and words arranged in thought units, as used by the speaker, are the basis for creating in the mind of the listener the ideas that the speaker has thought or is thinking. Inadequacy in this process is evidenced when the speaker's continuing thoughts are unrelated, interrupted, or inconsistent; when his statements are ambiguous, obscure in meaning, inexact, or incomplete, or contain grammatical errors; when his vocabulary is limited, inaccurate, or inexpressive; and when his pronunciations are noticeably incorrect or inaccurate often showing a lack of familiarity with the words he is using. Excellence in this process means that the speaker's thoughts are related, his statements clear and exact, and that his vocabulary is better than ordinary "hall-talk."

The process of phonation. This process includes the production and variation of tones of the voice and their pitch, intensity, duration, and quality, through which the speaker expresses variations in meaning.

Pitch refers to highness or lowness of tone.
Intensity refers to loudness of tone.
Duration refers to the length of time a tone lasts.
Quality refers to the individuality of the tone, its clearness, richness, and pleasantness.

The process of articulation. This process involves the modification of tones of the voice in forming the speech sounds while speaking. Speech sounds consist basically of vowels and consonants, which must be formed in continuous series correctly, accurately, and fluently if the listener is to understand easily what the speaker is saying.

Now, turn to *Assignment 2* in Section 29.

Essential skills of speech making. Occasionally, we find it necessary to speak in public. Public speaking requires the exercise of certain skills which go beyond those used in conversing. These skills, for purposes of study, are classified as follows:

Choice of subject. Selection of a general topic or field of knowledge to talk about to a specific audience.

Choice of thought. The selection and statement of one specific phase of a subject that can be adequately covered in the time allowed.

3

Choice of material. The selection of experiences, illustrations, examples, anecdotes, facts, opinions, or quotations to develop or amplify the specific thoughts selected.

Organization of material. The arrangement of thoughts and materials in a manner and order best suited to secure and hold the attention of the listeners, and to help them understand and remember what the speaker says.

Use of language. The selection of words and their arrangement into thought units to express the speaker's ideas.

Projection to the audience. The directness and enthusiasm with which the speaker presents and interprets the meaning of his thoughts. He must strongly stimulate the listener in order to gain and hold his attention and to cause him to respond appreciatively. The speaker's voice is important; his body must be alive with the full meaning—the ideas and feelings—of what he is saying to stir the listener to active participation in the situation and to insure complete and sympathetic understanding.

Control of bodily activity. Controlled posture, movements, and gestures while speaking. Such activity aids the speaker in focusing the attention of the listener on the ideas expressed. Bodily activity must be natural and must not call attention to itself. Some effective speakers use much bodily action; others use very little.

Rhythm. Fluency in speaking, appropriate individual rate of speaking, appropriate changes in the rate of speaking, and the use of pauses without noticeable jerkiness, interruptions, repetitions, or hesitations.

Pronunciation. Choice of the proper speech sounds and their appropriate combination into syllables and words which are spoken correctly and accurately, with stress upon the proper syllables.

Voice control. Control of pitch, intensity, duration, and quality of voice in the expression of meaning, in relation both to the ideas expressed and to the understanding of the listeners. Not all speakers who project well control their voices well.

Audience response. The reaction of the audience to the speaker and to the speech as a whole.

Next, see *Assignment 3* in Section 29.

Essential skills of reading aloud. It is difficult to estimate the number of times one may read aloud in public. But think of the oral reading you have heard—secretary's reports, children's poems and stories at home, scripture lessons at church meetings, entertainers at club meetings, or speakers on radio and television. Although the skills required for reading aloud and for public speaking are basically the same, each represents a different type of skill requiring special study and practice. The basic skills in reading aloud are as follows:

Choice of material. The choice of a suitable selection for reading to a specific audience.

Arrangement of material. The use of an appropriate introduction, and the use of appropriate transitional and connecting remarks to give unity to the material read. It includes cutting the selection if necessary.

Projection of thought. Interpretation of the thought content of the material to give a full understanding of its meaning to the listener.

Projection of emotion. Interpretation of the underlying spirit, mood, feeling, and emotional content of the material to insure an appropriate emotional response by the listener.

For control of bodily activity, rhythm, pronunciation, voice control, and audience response, see the corresponding sections above under Essential Skills of Speech Making.

Now, please turn to *Assignment 4* in Section 29.

Phonation. This is the production of voice. We consider your voice as parts of your skills in the essentials of speech making and reading aloud. Now let us think of it for itself. There are four elements which distinguish your voice from all others: your *pitch* (the highness or lowness of your voice), your *duration* (the length of time you hold a tone), your *intensity* (the loudness of the sounds you make), and your *quality*. In order to identify voice qualities which

5

are considered unpleasant or "unnatural," we use descriptive words such as the following:

1. *Muffled.* The tones and sounds seem to be produced in the throat. Make the sound "oo" as in the word "moot" several times. Then speak a sentence so that the tones of your voice sound as much as possible like *oo*, and you will have a sample of this type of quality. The tones seem to be throaty, dull, indistinct.

2. *Metallic.* The tones and sounds seem to originate in the mouth. Make the sound *ee* several times. Then speak a sentence so that the tones of your voice sound as much as possible like *ee*, and you will have a sample of this type of quality. The tones seem to be thin, flat, sharp, and without richness; they sound high in pitch. They may carry well but are somewhat unpleasant to hear.

3. *Nasal.* Too much nasal resonance, because the breath stream is directed mostly through the nose, rather than the mouth. The sound you make has a "humming" quality about it, somewhat like the "ma-ma" sound of a talking doll.

4. *Denasal.* A lack of nasal resonance. For amusement, you can exaggerate this quality by making all *m* sounds as *b*, and *n* sounds as *d*. Thus "moon" becomes "bood." "Noon" becomes "Dood."

5. *Harsh.* A raucous, unpleasant, unmusical voice whose tones are more like noises. In pitch the tones may be high or low.

6. *Hoarse-husky.* A voice which sounds as some voices do during or following a severe cold.

7. *Breathy.* Breathing noises, as in exhalation, are heard above the vocal tone. The individual may try to speak as he is inhaling.

8. *Infantile.* A baby voice used habitually by one of high school age or older.

Now, please turn to *Assignment 5* in Section 29.

Articulation. The production of speech involves breathing, phonation, resonation, and articulation. The last refers to the way you embellish your tones to form the identifying sounds of speech.

Finally, turn to *Assignment 6* in Section 29.

3   Now what?

Do you speak effectively? Few college freshmen do. The purpose of this course is to help you to achieve a style of speaking which is as *natural, correct,* and *effective* as possible *for you.* The pathways toward achieving this goal will vary with your needs and abilities, the condition of your speech mechanism, and the environment from which you have come. *In spite of limitations you can improve your speech.* There have been many instances of students who have become effective speakers in spite of initial inadequacies, poor equipment, and lack of experience.

The first step in improvement is for you to discover and recognize your needs and abilities as a speaker. We have tried to do this in the set of six items in your speech inventory. The second step is to become familiar with the goals you must attain and the pathways you must follow in attaining those goals. The third step is to supplant the old undesirable habits with new and more desirable ones through diligent practice and rehearsal before and after any speaking performance which you may have the opportunity to make. Your instructor will set up speaking experiences for you which will direct you toward the goals you should try to attain. *You must do the rest through your own unstinted effort.*

In addition, you should take the opportunity whenever possible of hearing good speakers and of speaking frequently yourself. If you are thus stimulated by others and stimulate yourself, your improvement will be more effectively facilitated. The stimulation received from hearing or making a *good* speech may exercise subtle and unsuspected but nevertheless marked influences on your future performances.

The *first principle* for you to learn is that there are no rigid, hard, and fast rules for speaking at all times. The principles stated in the following pages are submitted as *wise principles* to be followed in most speaking situations. You have a greater chance of becoming a successful speaker if you follow them than if you do not. *When you have become an experienced speaker, astute in audience analysis, an authority on your subject, and confident of your success, you may do as you please, but you probably will not find it necessary to for-*

sake the habits which practice in the use of these principles has engendered. You may rest assured that they are sound. They have stood the test of time as well as the scrutiny of scientists and artists.

Recognizing your needs and abilities. In the ratings your instructor made of your inventory performances, you will probably note more "4" ratings than any other. The reason is that "4" means adequate, and most people are about that.

Do not be surprised, however, if at the outset of this course you rate a "3" or a "2" in Adjustment to the Speaking Situation and Formulation of Thought (assignment 2), Choice of Thought, Organization of Material, and Projection to the Audience (assignment 3), and Arrangement of Material, Projection of Emotion, Voice Control and Audience Response (assignment 4).

Most students have very little trouble with the production of vocal tones or an acceptable quality, pitch, intensity, and duration. But about ten per cent of you will have an articulation inadequacy of the type studied in *Assignment 6*.

Goals in improving your speaking ability. This course is designed to help you improve. The next three major parts of this Handbook give detailed suggestions for improving the basic processes of speaking, the essential skills of speech making, and the essential skills of reading aloud. An understanding of these pages is part of your efforts to set up goals for your improvement. Following this expository material are many assignments. Each is designed with a specific goal or aim in mind. And in the procedure for each, an accounting is made of what has been learned before. By studying the textual material and by working toward the aim of each assignment, you will work out your goals for this course as you go along.

Do not be impatient. You cannot become an opera singer in ten easy lessons. Nor can you become a great speaker in a first course in speech. As a matter of good advice, you should not set any such goal for yourself anyway. Be assured that you *can* improve, that you *will* improve, that you will be a more effective speaker after this course is over than you are now. Let that much be your goal for the time being.

Establish new habits. Now, enjoy yourself with your class. If you have some ineffective habits of speaking, you will want to supplant them with new and better ones. That means to do the assignments as they are given. As stated before it is likely that you will get to know your classmates better here than in nearly any other course you ever take—because whenever anyone gives a good speech he tells a little bit more about himself, no matter what his topic.

PART TWO

The Basic Processes
of Speech

4   **What happens when we speak?**

The speech act. The term *speech* refers to the process or act of speaking. When normal, the act of speech is a total bodily response to a speaking situation of some kind. It is a single, coordinated muscular response to nerve impulses coming from the speaker's brain.

These nerve impulses occur as a result of thoughts and feelings which the speaker wishes to express in that speaking situation. His thoughts are expressed in words arranged in thought units and sentences. Each word is composed of selected speech sounds. Each speech sound evolves from the speaker's tone of voice at the moment. Listeners hear and react to the tone of his voice according to its pitch, intensity, duration, and quality. Appropriate variations in the pitch, intensity, duration, and quality of his natural tone of voice lend interpretation to his thoughts. Thereby, the listener becomes more fully aware of their logical and emotional meaning.

As the speaker formulates and utters his thoughts, natural bodily tensions, movements, and poses occur. As a result, the meaning and significance of his thought and feeling is more fully appreciated by the listener.

10

THE BASIC PROCESSES OF SPEECH

The speech mechanism. In speaking, the entire bodily mechanism is used. Certain parts of the mechanism, however, are especially important. They are: the breathing mechanism; the larynx containing the vocal cords; the cavities of the throat, mouth, and nose; the hard and soft palates; the tongue, the teeth, the lips, and the muscles of the face.

In a normal mechanism the teeth are properly occluded, and free from spaces between them. The tongue is normal in size for the mouth cavity, neither too large nor too small, and comparatively free in its movements. The hard and soft palates are normally developed. The latter is active in narrowing and closing the opening between the nasal cavity and the throat. The lips are properly formed so that they can close firmly to stop the breath and release it quickly and explosively, as necessary. The facial muscles are normally developed and free from paralysis or inactivity.

The functions of the speech mechanism and other bodily parts. To understand the functioning of the speech mechanism, it is especially important to note that, in addition to playing a vital part in the speech process, these parts of the mechanism have other more important bodily functions to perform. That they exist primarily to perform these other bodily functions should be recognized. Speech has sometimes been called an "overlaid" or "usurped" function.

The main function of the *breathing mechanism* is to get air into and out of the lungs to sustain life.

The chief functions of the *larynx* (*the voice box*) are to regulate the supply of air entering the lungs and to prevent bits of food or other foreign particles from entering the trachea or windpipe.

The *tongue, teeth, lips, palates,* and *facial muscles* function primarily in the taking in, chewing, and swallowing of food. The *mouth, nasal,* and *throat cavities* are passages through which air enters and leaves the body. Food also passes to the stomach through the mouth and throat cavities.

Many normal and abnormal but primary activities of these parts of the mechanism interfere with the speech act. These include: inhalation, chewing, swallowing, sneezing, coughing, hiccoughing, sobbing, laughing, sighing, and yawning. If you are speaking, for example, and suddenly need to sneeze, you will sneeze rather than speak. The primary function of sneezing takes over the mechanism at that moment.

Since the parts of the speech mechanism have these other primary bodily functions to perform, speech is, therefore, a secondary bodily function. The speech mechanism, thus, is subject to instability, and must be kept under constant control by the speaker.

Nerves and muscles must function as a unit. The neuromuscular (nerve and muscle) organization of the speech mechanism is very complicated. Many nerves share in carrying impulses to the muscle groups that are called into play when you speak. Not one muscle, but many cooperate in the speech act. The muscles are arranged in pairs, right and left, each being an exact copy of the other but reversed in position and action.

These pairs of muscles receive their impulses to act from several nerve fibres—the right from the left hemisphere of the brain, the left from the right hemisphere of the brain. Hence, for the speech act to be normal and at its best, nerve impulses and muscle actions must synchronize. They must operate together continuously. They must be integrated in their action. All muscles and nerves which participate in the speech act must function as a unit in perfect time order and balance. When this is not the case, speech inadequacies result.

What happens when you speak. As a result of conditions at the moment, you have thoughts and feelings to which you desire your listener or listeners to react. As you speak, these thoughts and feelings become meaningful to the listener through your words, tones, inflection, movements, gestures, and facial expressions. As you continue to express your thoughts and feelings, the following occur almost simultaneously.

1. Breath in varying degrees of pressure is sent up through your larynx.

2. Your vocal cords in the larynx adjust and readjust appropriately, modifying the outgoing breath into a series of breath waves.

3. Your throat, mouth, and nasal cavities and their openings assume, (a) coordinately, (b) momentarily, and (c) successively appropriate sizes and shapes to receive these breath waves and to amplify or build them up into the required vocal tones.

4. Next, these breath waves are further modified by your tongue, teeth, facial muscles, and lips to form the necessary speech sounds.

5. The breath waves, as now modified, are sent forth from your mouth and nose as sound waves and are transmitted through the air. (You have seen the ripples that occur when you drop a pebble into still water. The sound waves coming from your mouth and nose spread through the air in somewhat the same way.)

6. While your voice mechanism is sending forth these sound waves to the ears of your audience, bodily movements, gestures, and facial expressions are causing variations in the light waves that reach the eyes of your audience.

7. As the sound waves strike the eardrums of your listener, they are changed, through the mechanism of his ear, into a specific pattern of nerve energy. As this pattern of nerve energy reaches his brain it becomes meaningful to him, subject, of course, to the limitations of the sound waves as received by him and his capacity to interpret their meaning.

8. The light waves received by the eyes of the listener are also changed to a specific pattern of nerve energy which records an additional impression in his brain. The meaning of this impression is interpreted in relation to what he is hearing you say at the moment.

9. As a result of receiving these sound and light waves, the listener may exhibit behavior or specific reactions which you may observe and to which you may react as you speak.

Four fundamental processes. For purposes of study—training and retraining—the speech act is divided into four fundamental processes. These processes are:

Adjustment to the speaking situation
Formulation of thought
Phonation
Articulation.

These processes are the foundation of all forms of speaking activity —from conversation to formal oratory. They are treated in detail in the following pages.

5   **Adjustment to the speaking situation**

Adequacy in the processes of formulation of thought, phonation, and articulation is dependent upon the degree with which the speaker is mentally and emotionally adjusted to the speaking situation.

If you are well adjusted to the speaking situation you will possess a stable, well-integrated bodily mechanism, exhibit poise, balance, ease, naturalness, purposiveness. You are free from inhibitions, bodily tensions, and mannerisms. You speak coherently, fluently, emphatically.

If you are not well adjusted to the speaking situation you may possess an unstable, poorly integrated bodily mechanism, lack poise, be unbalanced, ill at ease, unnatural, tense, inhibited; your behavior may be purposeless; uncontrolled bodily mannerisms are apparent. You may be nervous, excited, frightened, hesitant, uncertain, chaotic, unable to speak coherently, fluently, emphatically.

If you are not well adjusted to the speaking situations when you face them, if your bodily mechanism is unstable, the other fundamental processes will be affected. You cannot, therefore, speak well. The following suggestions may aid you in becoming well adjusted to the speaking situation.

Understand what good speaking is.   Remember that the function of the speaker is communication, not display; that the audience wishes to hear and understand the speaker's ideas rather than to watch him speak and be impressed by his technique and extraordinary skill. The latter are always less important than communication. Good speaking is neither mechanical nor artificial; it possesses a quality of *naturalness*. Avoid the attitude that there is nothing interesting or worth while for you to talk about. You need not always speak on serious or profound subjects; you need not always present them in a serious and profound way. Choose subjects about which you already know a great deal. Your words need not be long or unusual, your gestures do not need to be elaborate or rehearsed. It is not necessary to use a certain type of posture or special hand and arm gestures, or to move about the platform methodically. You are not required to have a richly melodious voice that sings its words in perfect tone and cadence. Nor is it necessary for your pronunciation to be as fine as that of professional actors. You need not speak so fluently that there are no hesitations, repetitions, or uncertainties. Use that style of speaking which best accomplishes your purpose in the specific situation. There is no style of speaking suited to all occasions.

Understand the nature of the "speech act." As we said before, the speech mechanism is an unstable mechanism. You learned that, because of its very nature, it is subject to inconstancies. You also learned that the speech organs have more fundamental functions than speaking, and that these more fundamental functions take precedence over the "speech act" in sneezing, coughing, or being out of breath, for example.

Furthermore, the speech act is influenced by bodily and emotional states or disturbances. The functioning of the speech mechanism is affected by fear, excitement, anger, joy, sadness, surprise, fatigue, and so forth. Manifestations of emotional or bodily disturbances during the speech act include: breathing irregularities; stiff, unnatural posture and movements; uncontrolled muscle trembling, such as knees knocking or hands shaking; interruptions caused by swallowing, laughing, sighing, yawning, forgetting; frequent and prolonged hesitations; sudden and uncontrolled changes in pitch, loudness, rate of speech, and quality of tone; inaccuracy or indistinctness of the speech sounds.

You must and can learn through experience to keep control over your reactions to these various mental, emotional, and bodily states. Realize, however, that a perfect functioning of the mechanism during the speech act is not only rare but improbable. Even the best and most highly trained speakers experience some of the difficulties that you do.

Be realistic about yourself as a speaker. You may make an improved adjustment to the speaking situation by adopting a realistic point of view toward yourself as speaker. Know yourself. Find out the facts about yourself as a speaker. Appraise your talents. Do not think you are better than you are, but do not minimize your abilities. After your instructor has made a diagnosis of your speech needs and abilities in terms of the fundamental processes and the basic essentials of effective speaking, study the diagnosis. Become familiar with your weaknesses or inadequacies as well as with your strong points.

15

Then face the facts about yourself as a speaker. Accept the description of your speech needs and abilities as evidence of your present level of ability and use it as a starting point for your training. Avoid worrying about speaking situations that you have not been called upon to face, and forget past speaking experiences in which you have not been successful. Do not spend time daydreaming, wishing you were a better speaker than you really are, or pretending that you have acquired skills which in reality you have not. Instead, admit your inadequacies, but learn to emphasize your strong points and minimize your weaknesses. Succeed in spite of your handicaps. Accept criticism in a sincere, matter-of-fact way instead of feeling that you have been personally belittled. Remember that a recognition of one's own needs is the first step toward improvement. Adopt the following point of view: "I may not be an excellent speaker. In the beginning I may be a poor speaker with inadequacies, but I shall constantly strive to communicate my thoughts and feelings to my audience as naturally and directly as I possibly can, despite my limitations. With experience, I know that I shall improve."

Let individuality as a speaker be your goal. Strive to develop yourself as a speaker in terms of goals that are not only possible but probable for you to attain. Individuality as a speaker should be your first goal. Your heredity and environment have made you an individual. Be yourself! Do not try to copy exactly the style someone else uses; his style is *his* individuality expressing itself. Let *your* individuality express itself! There is no style of speaking that is suited to all persons; but, in developing your own style of speaking, do not ignore the principles of effective speaking about which you will learn in many assignments. Modify your own personal speaking style in accordance with them.

Make a speech at every opportunity. Seek opportunities to speak before audiences as often as possible. The best way to improve your adjustment to the speaking situation is through experience in speaking situations—all kinds of them. You may find at first that is it not easy, but you will also find that with each successive experience it will be easier, and soon you will begin to enjoy it. Speak about topics with which you are thoroughly acquainted, that arise out of your own background and experience. Sometimes you will be able to plan what you are going to say over a considerable period of time. At other times you will speak with little preparation. Whatever the circumstances, when the opportunity comes, *speak*, make your contribution. Concentrate on your ideas and what they mean, not on how you say them. You will find that it will be easiest, in the beginning, to recount experiences that you have had—easier for you because they are part of you and because the audience will be immediately interested. And make these talks short!

Do not expect to become well adjusted to the speaking situation immediately or be disturbed if your progress is slow and gradual. Set a series of goals for yourself that you can reasonably attain, so that you need not be dissatisfied nor unhappy with your progress.

Believe that stage fright is a natural, normal reaction. Difficulty in adjusting to the speaking situation is most frequently caused by stage fright, so called, but stage fright is the natural, normal attitude and reaction of the inexperienced speaker. If you are not an experienced speaker, you may feel nervous and uncertain about yourself and how well you will do. But you must recognize that experienced speakers have through their experience become poised, and confident that they can adjust to nearly any circumstance that may arise in speaking situations. You, too, can attain this poise and confidence through experience in speaking. It takes longer for some speakers to acquire it than for others. But you must speak often and in many kinds of speaking situations. Some of the following suggestions may help you.

1. Speak on topics about which you are well informed, on experiences that you yourself have had.

2. When you know that you have to make a speech, prepare well. Think about the topic, make notes, say it over to yourself. Have the notes with you. Use them if necessary.

3. If the speech conditions permit, introduce some object in the speech and talk about it and demonstrate it, or plan to use a blackboard diagram which you draw while talking about it.

4. Think about what you are going to say. Before you are called upon, say the first sentence to yourself. Say it to yourself as you go to the platform. As you take your position on the platform, repeat it to yourself, then take a deep breath, say, possibly, "Ladies and Gen-

tlemen," then say the prepared sentence aloud, and your speech has begun.

5. If you are excited and seem to tremble before being called upon, relax and breathe deeply to counteract the bodily tension which exists.

6. If you feel weak when you get to the platform, lean against something, perhaps. If your hands or knees tremble, touch them against the desk or lectern to stop the trembling, which, when stopped, usually does not begin again.

7. Move about the platform. Be active. Make yourself use gestures —any kind. An active body will help destroy the evidence of your fears and actually cause you to be more at ease.

6   Formulation of thought

The process of formulation of thought refers to the act of creating, arranging, and expressing thought while speaking. As a speaker converses he creates ideas, chooses and arranges words in thought units and sentences for their conveyance, and utters them, all as part of one act or process.

The speaker who is superior in formulation of thought states his thoughts coherently in a form that is adequate and essentially correct. He knows exactly what he is going to say and says it with economy of words and good taste. His thought is continuous, uninterrupted, consistent, logical; clear, exact, obvious. His vocabulary is broad; he uses simple, specific, colorful words; his sentences are grammatically correct and express each thought completely, exactly, emphatically; his words are pronounced acceptably.

The speaker who is inadequate in formulation of thought may lack coherence and consistency in his thinking and may use bad and incorrect forms in expressing his thoughts. He gives evidence of not knowing what he is going to say or how he is going to say it; he seems confused, uncertain, chaotic. His successive thoughts may be disjointed, unrelated, interrupted, repeated, inconsistent, illogical, contradictory, have no single end or goal; his statements may be obscure, inexact, and indefinite in meaning. His vocabulary may be limited, too simple, dull, ambiguous, vulgar, inexpressive; his sentences may be grammatically incorrect; his pronunciation may be noticeably inaccurate.

If you are no better than adequate in this process, you should aim to develop more skill in the formulation of thought. Skill in thought formulation gives "dignity" and "distinction" to the speech and the speaker. It is through effectiveness in the exercise of this function that you provide the basis for the projection of your ideas to your audience with precision, exactness, emphasis.

Formulation of thought and the speaking situation. Formulation of thought is most simply defined in terms of the informal, rather than the formal speaking situation. The informal speaking situation is characterized by conversation about or discussion of a subject by two or more interested persons, in which each makes a contribution as and when he desires. The formal speaking situation is characterized by the speaker-audience relationship, in which the speaker does all the talking for the benefit of the listeners. Thought, when expressed in either type of situation, should have a purpose in terms of and relevant to the situation at the moment of utterance.

For thought to be purposive in its creation the speaker must show that he has a knowledge of the drift of the points brought out in the immediate discussion; that he has a sufficient knowledge of the subject under discussion to make possible a contribution to it in the form of fact or opinion; that he has an interest in the subject and the discussion accompanied by a desire to contribute to it; an interest in knowing more about the subject under discussion as expressed in related questions; sufficient adjustment to the situation for the formulation and expression of thought to occur at its best; and a realization that when thought is expressed it must be formulated so that the listener may comprehend it.

For thought to be purposive in its formulation, the expression of it must show that it is complete, that is, the expression of a thought once begun must be completed without digression or interruption. It must be consistent, that is, the expression of the thought must observe logical order, the words must follow in sequence. It must not be contradictory. It must be continuous, that is, there must be no frequent interruptions, hesitation, and uncertainties resulting from not knowing what to say or what words to choose in expressing the

19

thought. It must be coherent, that is, details must be combined into a related whole. It must be clearly and specifically stated, free from abstraction and ambiguity. It must be correctly stated, free from error in grammatical structure. And finally, for thought to be purposive in its expression, the speaker should speak acceptably, that is, his pronunciation of the words in sequence must be adequate.

In the formal speaking situation the speaker must exercise greater skill in the principles mentioned above than in the informal speaking situation. He will show that he has a knowledge of and experience in public speaking. Surely he will be sufficiently well adjusted to the speaking situation to allow for a normal functioning of the bodily mechanism, thus facilitating the formulation and expression of thought.

7   Phonation

Characteristics. The process of phonation refers to the production and variation by the speaker of vocal tones—their pitch, intensity, duration, and quality. Pitch refers to highness or lowness of tone. Intensity is loudness. Duration is the length of time a sound lasts. Quality refers to the individuality of tone.

A speaker is superior in phonation when his voice has a basic quality which is clear, full, rich, resonant, mellow, pleasing, beautiful. It is more often medium or low in pitch. It is legato rather than staccato. It has a reserve of intensity. It is flexible, recording easily and without apparent effort the broadest and most subtle changes in thought and mood.

Voice inadequacies. In evaluating the speaker's adequacy in phonation, the skilled observer looks for the following inadequacies.

Organic inadequacies. Included may be:

1. Malformation of the nose, mouth, or throat cavities and the larynx.
2. Obstructions in the cavities, such as adenoids.
3. Chronic inflammations in these cavities and the larynx.

Pitch. Among possible inadequacies are:

1. Abnormally high or low pitch.
2. Lack of variation in pitch—vocal monotony.
3. Pitch patterns—rising or falling inflections regardless of meaning; identical inflections from phrase to phrase regardless of meaning.

Intensity. Inadequacies may include:

1. Abnormally loud or weak intensity.
2. Lack of variation in intensity, lack of emphasis.
3. Intensity patterns—the same variation in intensity regardless of meaning, for example, starting each sentence with more intensity than is used at its ending.

Duration. Among the possible inadequacies are:

1. Tones held for too short a time resulting in a staccato effect.
2. Tones held for too long a time resulting in an unpleasant drawl.
3. Lack of variability of rate of speech with all tones given about the same duration resulting in vocal monotony and lack of emphasis.

Quality. Types of inadequacies (which were more fully discussed in section 2) are as follows:

1. Muffled—too much resonance from the throat cavity.
2. Metallic—too much resonance from the mouth cavity.
3. Nasal—too much resonance from the nasal cavities.
4. Denasal—little or no resonance from the nasal passages.
5. Harsh—raucous, unpleasant.
6. Hoarse-husky—tense muscles in the mechanism, especially the throat, and possible unhealthy conditions in the cavities.
7. Breathy—the speaker's breath is heard above his vocal tones.
8. Infantile—has the characteristics of a young child's voice.

Flexibility. Lack of vocal flexibility is evidenced in monotony of pitch, intensity, duration, and quality in the speaker's expression of his meanings. The speaker seems to lack ability to control these vocal attributes as he speaks. His vocal mechanism is not necessarily inflexible. He simply does not make it function at its best, if at all.

Improvement. If you are found to be inadequate in any of these items you will want to attack your deficiency soon. Your instructor

21

may help outline a program of retraining for you, which will include many of the following bases for the improvement of phonation.

Hear your own voice. You must learn to hear your voice as others hear it. You should know its good characteristics and hear them. You should know its bad characteristics and hear *them* when they occur. Your ear should tell you when your voice is functioning at its normal natural best. A strong hearing sensitivity to the tones of your own voice is a first essential in voice improvement.

Your ear should hear in your own voice:

1. Its normal natural pitch level.
2. Its normal natural pitch range from the highest pitched sounds you make to your lowest.
3. Its pitch inflections upward and downward.
4. Its loud tones and its weak tones.
5. Its short, staccato, jerky tones, and its tones which drawl noticeably.
6. The various kinds of bad voice quality, such as nasal, muffled, and so on.

Relaxed mechanism. Your entire speaking mechanism should be relaxed, so to speak, while you are speaking. It should be free from abnormal muscle tenseness or tightness. A relaxed mechanism is the result of:

1. Good health, both physical and mental.
2. A proper understanding of what is expected of you when you speak, as we noted in considering adjustment to the speaking situation.
3. Confidence through familiarity with your general subject, and thorough preparation of the speech to be given.
4. Absence of stage fright and uncertainty, through experience in meeting speaking situations. The result of experience is a comfortable poise and a natural control of the functioning of the bodily mechanism during speech.

Normal pitch and pitch range. As you speak, the pitch of your voice fluctuates over a range of different pitches from low to high and high to low. Somewhere between the highest and lowest pitch your voice is capable of producing, there is a pitch level that is most natural for you. The pitch fluctuations of your voice seem to go up and down from this basic pitch level. You use it normally, when you are relaxed, at ease and not emotionally disturbed.

It is clear that the basic pitch level of men's voices is markedly lower than that of women. It has been said that the average pitch level of male voices is approximately 128 vibrations per second. The pitch level of female voices is approximately 256 vibrations per second, or about Middle C on the musical scale.

Some male voices are naturally lower or higher in pitch than others. The same phenomenon is true of female voices. Since there is a basic pitch level best for each individual, you must discover and make a habit of using that basic pitch level which is natural and best for you. In addition, you should discover your natural pitch range from lowest to highest and make the use of it habitual.

Many speakers, particularly among women, tend to use a higher pitch level than is natural for them. They tend also to use more high than low pitches in their pitch range, which usually is not natural for them either. The rule therefore is: speak at your natural pitch level and use your normal pitch range. *Your basic pitch level should be medium or low for you.* You should avoid too much use of the higher levels of your pitch range.

Reserve of intensity. You should have a strong voice. It should have a reserve of intensity that is not easily exhausted. You should have no trouble in making your audience hear in the average auditorium. To have a strong voice, you must:

1. Have a strongly active breathing mechanism. The muscles of respiration must act, during speech, with energy and power.

2. Cause a series of strongly vibrating breath waves to come from your larynx. These produce the pitches you desire.

3. At the same time, adjust the cavities of your throat, mouth, and nose with the breath waves.

4. Hold the adjustment of the cavities constant and continue the strongly vibrating breath waves until the tone has been built up by the resonance cavities to its full intensity.

8   Articulation

Characteristics. The process of articulation refers to the modification of the vocal tones, systematically, to form the speech sounds in connected oral discourse. The speech sounds consist in general of vowels, consonants, and diphthongs.

A speaker is superior in the process of articulation when the speech sounds are formed correctly, accurately, and fluently. Such a speech pattern is characterized by clear vowels and diphthongs, and precise articulation of the consonants, free from noticeable hesitations and interruptions. Precision, clarity, and beauty describe the speech pattern thus produced.

Articulation inadequacies. In diagnosing the adequacy of the process of articulation the skilled observer makes special note of the following:

Organic disorders: abnormalities of teeth, tongue, lips, palates, and face muscles.

Disorders of rhythm: stuttering, jerky, hesitant, uneven sound formation.

Disorders of sound formation: incorrect formation of certain of the speech sounds; inaccurate formation of vowels and consonants; slovenly articulation resulting from carelessness, inactivity of the articulators, or a rapid rate of utterance; foreign accent or dialect.

Improvement. If you are found to be inadequate in any of these items, you will want to correct your deficiency soon. Your instructor will help outline a program of retraining for you. Note the points outlined below as a basis for this retraining program.

Flexibility. You should have a flexible, active mechanism capable of making multitudinous, rapid, skilled movements. It has already been indicated that the tongue, lips, and soft palate should be active, flexible. Particularly should the lower jaw be active; it should be free from tension, loose.

Hearing. You should be conscious of and critical of the formation of your own speech sounds. You should be able to recognize deviations from the correct formation in the speech of others.

Correct speech sound formation. You should be able to form the consonants correctly. Consonants are vitally important to speech. They are largely responsible for its intelligibility and distinctness. A consonant is formed by a stoppage or interference with the outward moving breath stream in a specific manner to create a specific sound. Consonants are either voiceless (toneless) or voiced (toned). The vocal cords do not vibrate in the production of a voiceless consonant; vibration of the vocal cords is essential in the production of a voiced consonant.

The consonants are listed below. Note the italicized letters. You may wish to learn the International Phonetic Alphabet symbol for each consonant as indicated.

Voiced			**Voiceless**		
Symbol	Word	Phonetic transcription	Symbol	Word	Phonetic transcription
[b]	*b*it	[bɪt]	[p]	*p*it	[pɪt]
[d]	*d*in	[dɪn]	[t]	*t*in	[tɪn]
[g]	*g*et	[gɛt]	[k]	*k*it	[kɪt]
[z]	*z*oo	[zu]	[s]	*s*ue	[su]
[v]	*v*im	[vɪm]	[f]	*f*at	[fæt]
[w]	*w*et	[wɛt]	[ʌ]	*wh*et	[ʌɛt]
[ð]	*th*en	[ðɛn]	[θ]	*th*in	[θɪn]
[ʒ]	gara*ge*	[gərɑʒ]	[ʃ]	*sh*ed	[ʃɛd]
[dʒ]	*j*udge	[dʒʌdʒ]	[tʃ]	*ch*eap	[tʃip]
[m]	*m*e	[mi]			
[n]	*n*eat	[nit]			
[ŋ]	si*ng*	[sɪŋ]			
[l]	*l*ead	[lid]			
[r]	*r*ead	[rid]			
[h]	*h*id	[hɪd]			
[j]	*y*et	[jɛt]			

You should be able to form the vowel sounds correctly. Vowels give tonal quality or vocality to speech. A vowel is a voiced speech sound in which there is little interference with the outgoing air. Each different vowel when properly formed is the result of an integrated adjustment of the cavities of the mouth, throat, and nose and their openings to the vocal cord vibrations. This adjustment must be sustained momentarily for the intensity and richness of the sound to be built up. The most common vowel sounds used in general American speech are listed below.

Symbol	Word	Phonetic transcription	Symbol	Word	Phonetic transcription
[i]	eat	[it]	[u]	boom	[bum]
[ɪ]	it	[ɪt]	[ʊ]	book	[bʊk]
[e]	agent	[edʒənt]	[o]	omit	[omɪt]
[ɛ]	met	[mɛt]	[ɔ]	law	[lɔ]
[æ]	at	[æt]	[ɑ]	alms	[ɑmz]
[ə]	above	[əbʌv]	[ʌ]	buck	[bʌk]

You should use clear vowels. Allow time for the vowel to form, to secure the desired intensity and quality. Avoid muffling the vowel sounds by failure to open your mouth sufficiently to allow unimpeded emission of the modified breath stream.

The diphthong is made up of two vowels so closely blended that they lose their identity as individual sounds and become instead a new sound. The following diphthongs are used in general American speech. Check with your instructor as you make each sound, being sure that you understand the regional variations that you may have.

Symbol	Word	Phonetic transcription	Symbol	Word	Phonetic transcription
[eɪ]	maim	[meɪm]	[oʊ]	show	[ʃoʊ]
[ɑɪ]	ice	[ɑɪs]	[aʊ]	how	[haʊ]
[ɔɪ]	boy	[bɔɪ]	[ju]	mute	[mjut]

Accuracy. You should utter the sounds, as combined in words, with sufficient accuracy to insure adequate reception by the listener. Take time in forming the consonants in their relation to other sounds to allow for adequate formation. Use an equal distribution of breath; avoid the habit of using more breath force at the beginning than at the end of a word. You should, when required, be able to make a firm closure with an accompanying quick release of the blocked air. Avoid allowing too much breath to escape, which results in noisy or hissing sounds.

You should overcome lack of precision in articulation by avoiding certain common errors. For example, you should avoid talking too rapidly, more rapidly than the ease and accuracy of adjustment of your mechanism will allow. Avoid slurring—running sounds, syllables, or words together—[ʍəzæt] (what's that?), [dəwanə] (don't want to). Avoid weakening or eliminating final consonants such as [slɛp] (slept), [artɪs] (artists), [hæn] (hand), [faɪ] (five).

You should avoid lack of precision in articulating the middle consonants. Don't slur—[ənɜ˞stæn] (understand), [gʌvɜ˞mənt] (government), [ædʒətɪv] (adjective). Don't give tone to voiceless consonants—[wɔdə˞] (water), [ɪndəmədlɪ] (intimately), [bæbdɪst] (Baptist). Don't make voiced consonants voiceless—[bɪsnɪs] (business), [tris] (trees). You will notice the symbols [ɜ˞] and [ə˞] in the above. They are sometimes called "semi-vowels." They are formed by producing the sound of the vowel [ɜ] or [ə], and adding an [r] characteristic to each.

Fluency. As you speak, you should utter and combine the sounds fluently, rhythmically. Speech is not composed of separate sounds, but is an integration, in a necessary order and relationship, of sounds into syllables, syllables into words, and words into thought units. Repetition of, hesitations between, abnormally rapid or slow, unusually precise or inaccurate utterance of sounds, syllables, and words makes for a jerky, uneven, discontinuous speech pattern, which may be difficult to understand and unpleasant to listen to. It is comforting to know that all speakers will have non-fluencies at times.

PART THREE

The Essential Skills
of Speech Making

Introduction

Goals of speech making.   Speech making is a specialized form of speaking in which one individual presents his thoughts or the thoughts of another on a given subject to a group of listeners for their benefit or for the benefit of himself or the benefit of a cause. His immediate goal may be one or all of the following:

1. To inform or instruct.
2. To secure belief or action through persuasion.
3. To entertain or amuse.

Burdens of the speaker.   Regardless of his goal, the speaker must assume four fundamental burdens:

1. He must gain the attention of the audience and interest them in himself and his subject.
2. He must hold their attention and interest in spite of factors that may cause attention and interest to lag or fluctuate.
3. He must make his ideas clear to his audience in order that they may understand his thoughts exactly.

4. He must make them remember his thoughts and their relation one to another and to the central thought of his speech.

Essential skills of speech making. To accomplish the above, skill in the essentials of speech making is required. These essentials are: 1. Choice of Subject, 2. Choice of Thought, 3. Choice of Material, 4. Organization of Material, 5. Use of Language, 6. Projection to the Audience, 7. Control of Bodily Activity, 8. Rhythm, 9. Pronunciation, 10. Voice Control, 11. Audience Response.

Definitions of these essentials and principles involved follow.

9   Choice of subject

Suited to the audience. Select a general subject that is suited to the specific audience to which you will speak. Analyze your probable audience to determine their interests. Select this general subject only after you have ascertained all the facts you can about them and the situation. Remember, first of all, that your audience is composed of human beings. They must be interested if you wish them to attend to what you have to say. Remember, also, that you *can* interest them if you will.

In selecting your subject, ask yourself the following questions and be guided by the answers you make to them.

1. What will be the probable age range of my listeners?
2. Are my listeners likely to be intelligent, educated, and cultured —or otherwise?
3. What common interests are my listeners likely to have?
4. Will my audience be male, female, mixed?
5. What are my listeners likely to know about me? Will they be likely to have confidence in me when speaking on the subject I choose?
6. Why will the audience to which I will speak have gathered? Will it have gathered to commemorate some special day or event, to decide upon a course of action, to be inspired, to be informed, to be entertained?
7. What will my audience be likely to expect? What subject would it probably like to hear discussed?
8. What will be its probable mood, state of mind, attitude, de-

sire? Will it be boisterous, enthusiastic, docile, indifferent, anxious, drowsy? Will it be prejudiced, or free from prejudice?

9. What event or events have taken place recently that have gained general interest, approval, or disapproval?

10. What type of subject will my audience consider worth while listening to? This question does not imply that it is necessary for you to speak on weighty topics. It simply is a warning that your audience will be pleased only if the time spent in listening to you has been time profitably spent.

Suited to the speaker. Select a general subject that is suited to you, the speaker. It *should come from a background with which you are intimately familiar.* You should be an authority on each subject you choose to speak upon. Never forget this principle.

Any subject you choose should be one in which you are vitally interested. You may have had experiences related to it. You may enjoy reading about it. You may enjoy discussing it or telling others about it.

Give the type of speech which your judgment and experience tell you that you can give most successfully. Don't choose a subject unless you are reasonably sure you can make a success of it with the specific audience to which you will speak. Don't disappoint your audience by a poor choice of subject.

For mature speakers, facing speaking situations arising from their business, community, or family activities, choice of subject is usually not a problem. The immediate situation, the speaker's interests, his knowledge, his attitudes, his feelings, his desire to or the necessity for him to present his ideas will determine the subject upon which he speaks. But in your speech class, what subject to choose may seem to be quite a problem. However, you really do have quite a range of subjects to choose from, as indicated by the following list of possibilities.

1. Your subject may concern your vocation—your job, your studies.

2. It may concern your avocation—your hobbies in sport, science, nature, religion, art, collecting, writing, reading, speaking.

3. It may be an explanation and description of an event, an invention, a law, a process, a philosophy, a game. If you choose a subject of this type your success will depend upon your ability to be clear as well as interesting.

4. It may be a presentation and discussion of an experience or a series of experiences which you have had.

5. It may be a discussion of something you have read. If you choose this type of subject, *discuss* what you have read, rather than merely report the content of a book, magazine article, news story.

6. It may be a discussion of an individual, contemporary or historical, an evaluation of his life or an event in his life, an evaluation of his achievement.

7. It may be a belief that you hold or an opinion that you wish to support.

8. It may be the expression of a desire, a hope, a wish, a prophecy, the discussion of which will stamp you as original, a leader of thought, and as a consequence give you great satisfaction.

9. If you are a humorist, if you are clever in the use of language, if you are skilled in the development of comic situations, if you can present the humorous side of life *humorously* and with a point, do not hesitate to choose such a subject.

Do not make choice of subject for your class speaking assignments difficult. Almost anything within your experience will serve you well. Just be sure that it is sufficiently vivid and meaningful to make the speech easy to present to others with spontaneity, clarity, and interest.

10   Choice of thought

Central thought. Select from your general subject a specific phase of that subject, a central thought or main idea embodied in it, upon which you wish to dwell, that you wish your audience to consider in detail. The reasons for choosing a central thought are: to narrow the subject; to define its limits; to allow for concentration in order to give unity, coherence, and emphasis to the speech; to make your goal or purpose clear to the audience.

Requirements of central thought. The central thought of your speech should meet the following requirements:

1. It should be an all-encompassing statement of the goal you wish to attain in your speech. It should be the main point upon which

you wish your audience to focus their attention. It should be the main reason why you desire them to believe or do a certain thing.

2. All the thought and material to be included in your speech should be subordinate to it.

3. Its extent, the amount of thought and material it encompasses, should be proportionate to the time allotted to you by those requesting your appearance as a speaker. Ascertain this time limit before you prepare your speech. Your central thought should be sufficiently limited and narrow to be completely developed within the time allowed. It should not be so broad that it cannot be completely developed within the time you are allowed.

Statement of central thought. The statement of the central thought should conform to the following:

1. It should contain one thought and one thought only.

2. It should be stated in the form of a complete sentence. It may be stated in declarative form, for example: "I want to outline for you the functioning of a football team in executing the 'Statue of Liberty' play." It may be stated in the form of a question, for example: "What is a good recipe for making fudge?"

3. It should be a specific statement. It should be short and simple, rather than long and involved. It should be instantly intelligible to, easily understood by, the audience. It should be easily remembered by the audience. It should stimulate and arouse the immediate interest of the audience.

Nature of thought for speeches. The thought process which you use in the development of your subject will depend upon what you expect to accomplish with your audience as indicated by your central thought. Your thought pattern may be of three basic types:

1. To inform. The nature of your thought may be to give information, to make clear that which may not be clear to your audience. You may use any or all of the following devices: You may use *exposition,* in which you explain and amplify your thoughts, change the unfamiliar into the familiar, bring about understanding of terms, facts, things, points of view, beliefs, processes, organizations. You may use *narration,* in which you recount experiences, events and

stories, real, fictional, biographical. You may use *description*, in which you tell how that which is to be described affected your senses, how it looked, smelled, tasted, sounded, felt.

2. To persuade. Your plan may be to follow the sequence of persuading, in which case you endeavor to influence your audience "to believe or act as you wish them to believe or act." You assume a burden of proof, you presume opposition, you "state your case, then prove it." You must take a definite position, for or against a proposition. You must not straddle the issue, you cannot favor both sides. You must appeal to the reason, the intelligence of your audience. You must choose and present arguments that are very valuable in proving the soundness and expediency of your central thought. You must also appeal to the feelings, the emotions, the wants, the likes and dislikes of your audience if you expect to be persuasive. By relating your appeal both to the reason of your audience, and to their feelings and emotions, you are more certain to gain the desired result. Any appeal to reason that is not also an appeal to a want is seldom effective. Some of the common feelings and wants are love, fear, hate, patriotism, devotion, pity, sympathy, cleanliness, morality, comfort, security, ownership, efficiency, social esteem, pride, honor, right, duty, power.

3. To entertain. The nature of your thought may be to amuse, to entertain, to thrill, to while away the time of the audience in a pleasant, stimulating manner. What you present must actually amuse, entertain, thrill. The central thought of this type of speech is your immediate goal, the amusement and entertainment of your audience. The thought process used in the development of such a central thought are the stories, the incidents, the circumstances which you relate.

Subordinate points. Analyze your central thought. Break it up into its elements, its component parts, its subordinate points. Group your knowledge relative to your central thought into natural and inherent, not artificial, units. Each unit should be a subdivision of the central thought, a subsidiary idea or thought, a subordinate point. Be guided by the following suggestions. There must be more than one subdivision or point. Each point should develop the central thought directly. Each point should include a single thought. There

33

must be no overlapping. The points taken together should completely develop the central thought.

Audience analysis. Analyze your audience in terms of your central thought. Estimate their probable knowledge relative to it and their probable capacity for comprehension of it. Consider their probable interest in it, their prejudices toward it.

Selection of subordinate points. Evaluate the subordinate points of your central thought for the purpose of selecting those which must be presented to your audience. The points you wish to present may vary with the composition of your audience. Select those points which are essential to the development of the basic aspects of your central thought, which are necessary to insure comprehension by your audience, and are likely to be of most interest to the audience. Eliminate all points which are not vital to the complete development of your central thought and which are not essential in securing the interest or comprehension of your audience. Avoid using too many points. The audience can remember and absorb five or six, but not many more. The use of too many points is usually the result of poor analysis of your central thought or the choice of one that is too broad.

Statement of subordinate points. Formulate each subordinate point in a stimulating, concise, specific statement. Each point should be stated in the form of a complete sentence. Each point should be stated clearly, specifically, not generally. Each should be simple, easily understood, easily remembered. Each should be stated so that it may be easily distinguished from each other point. At times, statement of points in parallel form is a good thing.

11   Choice of material

Develop subordinate points. The central thought and its subordinate points must be developed, amplified, enlarged upon, and emphasized in order to insure interest, understanding, and belief on the part of the audience. The types of material to be used are dependent upon the nature of the central thought, and its subordinate points, and the audience to which the speech is to be presented. The types of material listed below should be used as indicated when necessary.

Explanation. The development and emphasis of your thought may be accomplished by explaining or translating for your audience the meaning and significance of your ideas, by simplifying, explaining, interpreting, restating. You simply talk *about* your idea. For example, you may clarify your thought, unfold its meaning by restating it in simpler words or forms. You may outline or list the characteristics of your thought, its essential aspects, thus distinguishing it from others, and making its meaning and significance clear. You may split your thought into its parts or elements in order to simplify it and make it clear. Or you may make your thought clear by commenting upon the derivation, or the root, or the source of unfamiliar words or terms.

Specific instances. The development and emphasis of your thought may be accomplished by relating specific instances or circumstances within your experience and the experience of the audience which illustrate the points you wish to make clear. Be certain that each instance or circumstance has a point, the point in question, and be certain that you make that point clear. For example, you may relate one or more personal experiences. Or you may tell a story or a series of stories, humorous or serious, which you have read or heard. Or you may set up hypothetical situations based on truth or fiction.

In relating experiences, stories, events, hypothetical situations, select carefully the details to be presented. Use only those details which are essential to the development of the point involved in each story, instance, or circumstance and which are necessary to give it its proper setting, color, flavor.

Comparison and contrast. The development and emphasis of your thought may be accomplished by use of comparison and contrast. You may compare and contrast ideas, objects, mechanical devices, principles, policies, theories, philosophies, persons, etc. For example, you may make your point clear by indicating its similarity or likeness to something familiar or known to the audience. Or you may make your point clear by indicating its dissimilarity or unlikeness in the same way. Choose that material which is best suited to simple, natural, direct, exact, fair comparison or contrast and which is especially helpful in making your point. Avoid complicated and remote comparisons.

Statistics. The development of your thought may be accomplished by the use of statistics. In establishing your point, use statistics that are incontrovertible and authoritative. They must not be based on rumor or hearsay. Use statistics your audience can comprehend. The mere use of figures does not guarantee comprehension or belief. If your statistics are difficult for the audience to visualize or comprehend, incorporate them in examples or accompany them with simple, familiar illustrations. Be exact in your statement of the statistics you present. Put them on a note card and read them verbatim, if necessary. Usually, it is best to quote your statistics in round numbers. For example, quote $1,592,871.61 as $1,593,000 or $1,600,000, depending upon the need for exactness. It is wise to state the source of your statistics, the authority, the name of the publication, the publisher, the date of publication, the page reference.

Interpret the meaning of your statistics as they relate to the point you wish to make. Apply them to the point. Make them meaningful. Your audience may not remember the statistics you quote but they should remember the point they develop.

Opinion. The development of your thought may be accomplished by the use of opinions, interpretations, conclusions, and beliefs of yourself and others. Opinions are not facts, and they are not necessarily true statements. Their value depends upon the competence and reputation of the person who makes them. You may state your own opinions if they are the result of careful thought and not merely hasty generalization. You should be able to give reasons and supporting evidence for your opinion if necessary. You may state the opinion of a friend if he is competent to express an opinion on the point in question. Or you may state the opinion of an authority or several authorities on the point in question. In this case, be sure the authority is especially competent, a thorough student of the subject upon which he is quoted. He should be a well-known man of good reputation for his testimony to be readily acceptable to the audience. If he is not well known but is competent it may be necessary to establish him as competent. He must be unbiased, free from prejudice, for his opinion to be reliable and valid. If you quote the opinions of authorities, quote them exactly. It is better to read the quotations verbatim from a note card. State the source of the opinion quoted, the authority, the name of the publication, the publisher, the date of publication, the page reference.

Interpret the significance of your opinions and the statements from authority which you quote as they relate to the point you wish to make. Apply them to the point, make them meaningful.

Amount of material.   Choose material that will develop each subordinate point fully, adequately, and completely. Do not choose more material than the development of each point demands. The amount necessary should be determined by the nature of the point and the specific audience to which you speak. Do not use more details than you can reasonably expect your audience to assimilate and comprehend in the time allowed. Your audience may become confused if you use too many details, facts, or illustrations. If you use too much material you may not have time to relate it properly to the point and to the central thought of your speech, to adapt it adequately to your audience. A multitude of details may obscure your point.

Do not rely on an insufficient amount of material in the development of your points. You cannot expect to be clear and effective nor accomplish your objective if your material is too limited. If your points are not fully developed, or if your ideas lack support and substantiation, your speech is likely to be all talk—"hot air," as is sometimes said. Your audience will accuse you of having nothing to say, of not knowing your subject, and so will become bored and not listen. Your speech will be trite, ordinary, uninteresting, inconsequential. With too little material you may be guilty of an unpardonable sin—hasty generalization.

If you need material.   If you need more material for developing your points, you must change the central thought of your speech or find the needed material. To change the central thought of your speech is often the most advisable thing to do in such a case. If the subject had developed out of a background with which you were familiar, you would not be faced with the necessity of finding more material. You should never choose a subject for a speech unless material for its development is readily available.

Or try to accumulate concrete, specific material to develop your central thought if you feel that you need it. However, avoid the common error of using but one source for all of your material. Recall related experiences that you have had and select those that may be useful in developing your points. Discuss your subject with friends for purposes of gathering illustrations and opinions. Consult recognized authorities, in person, for source material or specific information and examples. Examine the current newspapers and magazines for recent information, examples, statistics, opinions. Visit the library. Consult the librarian. Look in general reference books, encyclopedias, *The World Almanac,* and others. Consult the *New York Times Index, The Reader's Guide,* for references to comparatively recent materials in the newspapers and magazines. Also, use the library card index to locate books related to your subject.

Relevant, reliable, consistent, convincing material. Choose relevant, reliable, consistent, convincing material for the development of your points. Also, be sure to interpret accurately the material you choose. Do not let prejudices, likes, and dislikes influence you in the choice or interpretation of your material. Choose only relevant material—material directly related to your point. Beware of using irrelevant, unrelated material. Keep on the point—don't wander from it. Choose only the most reliable material—material that the audience will accept without question. Is it hearsay, rumor, gossip? Does it come from reliable sources? Is it ethical for you to ask your listeners to accept it? It is folly to choose and present questionable material in the development of your points. Choose only material which is consistent, compatible. For example, it must be in accord with (not inconsistent with), and logically develop the point in question. It must be in agreement with, not contradict materials used elsewhere in your speech. If presented as factual, it must not be inconsistent with fact or reality. Each separate bit of material must be logically consistent, coherent.

Suited to your audience. Choose material in the development of your points that is suited to your probable audience. Choose your material only after a careful analysis of that probable audience, as follows:

1. *For interest.* Choose material that will create the greatest possible interest on the part of your audience, so that it will catch their

attention immediately. Choose material closely related to the experience of your audience. Choose material that is related to human motives and desires such as money, power, reputation, happiness, honor, right, or duty. Remember that your audience is composed of human beings. Human beings are, basically, much the same. You will fail if you talk over the heads of your audience, by using abstract and impersonal material.

Choose material that has inherent attention values, which by its very nature gets attention. Use novel and striking rather than ordinary, commonplace, inconsequential materials. Choose material that will arouse the curiosity of your audience. An audience that is curious will not be difficult to keep interested. Choose material that will aid you in creating in your audience a feeling of suspense. Develop in them a state of mental apprehension and anxiety about what you have to say. The suspense factor when properly used is a great asset to a speaker. Choose material which has an aspect of the sensational. Here, you may use startling but well-founded material. You are warned, however, to be reasonable. Don't be an alarmist.

Whenever possible, choose humorous material to accompany the more weighty and serious material. If your subject lends itself to the introduction of humor, avail yourself of the opportunity. Don't be too serious. Remember that "A bit of nonsense, now and then, is relished by the wisest men." A wise selection of humor makes for a pleasant response on the part of the audience. It may reduce undesirable tensions, provide relaxation, and increase the friendliness, interest, and attention of the audience. But be sure that the humor is suited to your subject and audience and is applicable to the point you are making.

2. *For clarity.* Choose material for the development of your points that will aid you in being clear. You will fail if you allow your audience to become hazy, perplexed, uncertain, as to what you mean. What you have in mind should always be self-evident from the material you use. Be clear, through wise choice of material. Choose vivid, colorful material. Picture your thoughts plainly. Generally, for most audiences, it is wise to use illustrations, examples, comparisons, contrasts freely. Create vivid images, set them out in bold relief; use brilliant, broad, bold strokes. More often than not, most of your

speech should consist of illustrative material. It is the most important factor in being clear.

Choose simple rather than complicated material. It is better to be easy to understand than hard to understand. In the latter case, you are more often likely to be misunderstood. Choose only that material which is within the range of the experience and the imagination of your audience. Don't talk "over the heads" of your audience, by using material which is far removed from everyday life. When possible, choose illustrative material which has aspects of the familiar. Secure understanding from the audience by proceeding from things that they know about to the new ideas you want them to have. Lead them into an understanding and appreciation of the new through relating it to the old.

Assimilate, adapt, interpret your material. Make your speech a worthwhile representation of your own work. Your contribution to your audience is based upon what you do with your material after you have chosen it. Study your material, digest it, assimilate it. Rework it so that it represents a real part of your own knowledge. Think about its application to your subject and your audience. Your job is only partly done when you have chosen your material.

Adapt your material to your central thought, points, and audience. Relate it to the central thought, and the points which you use. Actually use your material to develop your central thought. Do not let the audience supply relationships. Too many speakers simply report facts, statistics, opinions, without interpreting their meaning. A report of an event, a trip, the content of a news story or magazine article is not a speech as properly conceived. Do not be merely a reporter, a statistician, a walking encyclopedia. Do not give the audience the idea that you have nothing to offer but a dry statement and classification of facts. You will fail if you do not interpret, evaluate, apply, and structuralize your material in a way that makes it have extraordinary significance for the immediate audience.

12   Organization of material

You must organize your thought and material *for* your probable audience. You must structuralize it so that they may visualize it as a whole, always seeing its parts as they relate to the whole. You will thus implant in the minds of your audience your central thought, its subordinate points, and the material used in their development. If you organize your thought and material well, your audience will follow your presentation easily and without effort. You will be readily understood, and your thought will be easily remembered. Time spent in organizing thought and material is well worth while.

Organization formula. The organization of your speech may be accomplished best by establishing four parts, each having a distinct function. These four parts are *Introduction, Central Thought, Body,* and *Conclusion.* The parts may vary in length and importance with the type of subject and the type of audience, but the four functions remain the same for all speaking situations.

1. The introduction. Your introduction should lead your audience up to a consideration of the central thought of your speech. It should "dispose" the audience favorably toward you. It should establish a common ground between you and your audience. It should establish in your audience a mental set, a state of mind, a receptive attitude, toward the central thought under consideration. You should *arouse* the attention and *stimulate* the interest of your audience.

In addition to the above, you may need, depending upon your central thought and your audience, to accomplish special functions in your introduction. It may be necessary for you to establish your right to address your audience on the subject chosen. In some cases you may need to give a history of your subject, give definitions of unfamiliar terms, and consider other necessary items. It may be necessary for you to remove prejudices, allay suspicion, and promote open-mindedness.

Length of introduction. The length of your introduction will vary with your central thought and your audience. If your audience is unfamiliar with or prejudiced toward you or your subject, or both, more time undoubtedly must be spent in your introduction than if the situation were otherwise. In general, a long speech requires a longer introduction than does a short speech. As someone has said, "The introduction should be short enough to be interesting and long enough to cover the subject." Some introductions have been no longer than one sentence.

Type of introduction. The type of introduction to use depends upon your central thought and audience. In any case, select that type of introduction which is most appropriate. It may consist of one or several of the following approaches: (1) You may make remarks concerning yourself, refer to some experience of yours. (2) You may refer to the occasion, the audience, or the reason for the meeting. (3) You may refer to the subject, its timeliness, its importance. (4) You may build up a dramatic situation as a means of establishing a background for the development of your central thought. (5) You may embody your introductory thoughts in suitable illustrations. (6) You may tell a story or a series of stories, humorous or serious, which embody your introductory thought and establish a background for the development of your central thought. Do not "drag in" funny stories for the sole purpose of making the audience laugh. Be sure that each story you use is appropriate to the subject and audience, and that each story has a point. Be sure that you clearly relate the point of your story to what you are trying to accomplish in your introduction.

In preparing your introduction beware of giving the audience credit for knowing either more or less about your subject that it does; beware of telling stories not bearing upon the subject; of leading the audience to expect considerations not forthcoming, thereby giving them a false idea of your goal; dampening interest and destroying confidence by making apologies; using an introduction which is too long.

2. Central thought. (See *Central Thought* under *Choice of Thought*, Section 10.) You should state your central thought at the end of the introduction and before you begin the body of the speech in which its subordinate points are to be developed. You should state your central thought more than once during the course of the speech. You may repeat it verbatim, state it in other words or another form, amplify and enlarge upon it simply and briefly. Be certain that your audience knows exactly what you are talking about. State your central thought at least three times.

On the other hand, some experienced speakers, when they face a peculiar speaking situation, may find it advisable to omit the statement of the central thought altogether. Before an uncertain or hostile audience it may be advisable to withhold for a time the statement of the central thought. If the speaker elects to omit the statement of it, the speech must be so well developed that it is established by implication. Omission of the central thought statement does not mean that the speaker has no central thought—only that the statement is omitted. Inexperienced speakers should beware of omitting the statement of it.

3. The body. The function of the body of the speech is the development of your central thought in such a way that it interests your audience, is clearly and emphatically presented, and as a consequence is generally understood and remembered by them. The central thought should be developed as a unit, as a whole. Subordinate points and materials must stand out only as they relate to the development of the central thought. The importance and the necessity of the following suggestions will vary with the intelligence of the audience and its knowledge of your central thought, and hence its ability to follow and absorb your thought and material.

All points should be subordinate to the central thought and presented so that the audience is aware of how each develops it directly. As you develop each point, state what it accomplishes and how it is related to the central thought. Incorrect inferences and relationships by your audience are thus prevented. Repeat each point and its relation to the central thought as you proceed to the following point. The audience is thus less likely to forget your points, more likely to remember them. Use transitions, relating the point completed to the point following. Your audience is thus certain to be carried from one thought to another without misunderstanding.

Development of subordinate points. Each subordinate point should be developed as a unit, as a whole. Materials used in the development of a point should stand out only as they relate to the development of that point and the central point. All materials should

43

be subordinated to the point in process of development and presented in such a way that the audience is aware of how each bit of material develops that point directly. As you present each bit of material, state what it accomplishes in the development of that point. Avoid using disconnected but related materials from which the audience must infer relationships. You should supply the necessary connection. If you do not, the audience may make the wrong inference or make none at all. As you complete the development of each point, briefly review, summarize the materials presented, and state their application to the point in question.

Your materials should be handled so that the important details and the important relationships are remembered by the audience. For example, you should repeat the names of persons, places, things, dates, statistics, statements of authorities, complicated formulae, mechanical processes, or specific directions, if you wish them to be remembered. You should repeat a statement if its meaning is dependent upon a single word or a single syllable of a word. Repeat several times in the same or different words any detail or statement you wish to emphasize, which you wish your audience to remember. If you are not sure that you have made yourself clear, or that the audience has assimilated the details of your material, do not hesitate to repeat and restate until you are certain that the audience visualizes and understands.

Arrangement of subordinate points. You should arrange your subordinate points, depending upon the central thought and the immediate audience, in an order best suited to insure the greatest understanding and the least confusion. Plan the best arrangement in advance even though conditions in the audience may make it necessary to change the order of arrangement of your points at a moment's notice, before or after you have begun speaking. Always arrange your points systematically in terms of your goal, as defined by your central thought, which you have set to accomplish with your specific audience. Avoid a random, wandering, unsystematic arrangement of points.

It may be wise to arrange your points logically, having each succeeding point built upon and dependent upon the development of the former. In the development of a central thought which entails a great deal of exposition and description this arrangement may be best. It may be necessary in persuasive and argumentative speaking with some thoughts and with some audiences.

It may be wise to arrange your points chronologically, having events follow a time order. Chronological order of arrangement is mandatory in the development of a central thought which must be treated in an historical manner.

It may be wise to arrange your points in climactic order, in which the most important and strongest, the most stimulating point occurs last. In narration, climactic order may be not only wise but necessary. In persuasive and argumentative speaking, the composition of the audience and the mental state of its members will be the determining factors in the use of climactic order of arrangement. With some audiences it may be wise to present the strongest and most important point first.

Arrangement of material for subordinate points. You should arrange the material to be used in the development of each of the subordinate points in the order best suited to the development of that point in terms of the immediate audience to which you are speaking. What has been said above, regarding the arrangement of the subordinate points, can also be applied to the arrangement of the material in the development of each point. In most cases the following form is advisable, depending upon the amount and kind of material at your disposal. It is especially recommended for the developing of points in persuasive speaking. In most cases the following form is advisable, depending upon the amount and kind of material at your disposal:

1. Begin with a statement of the point to be made, followed by

2. A restatement of the point in another and perhaps simpler form to insure comprehension and emphasis, followed by

3. Introductory material, needed explanation and definition of terms, followed by

4. General illustrations, followed by

5. More specific illustrations, followed by

6. Statements from authority, followed by

7. Summary, restatement, application and transition, in which you emphasize the point completed by reviewing its development, relating and connecting it to the thesis and that which follows.

45

4. The conclusion. Your conclusion should effectively and force-fully leave the central thought of your speech with your audience. It should restate and enforce the most important elements of your speech and relate them to your central thought, integrating it with the motives and interests of your audience.

The type or kind of conclusion you use will vary with your central thought and immediate audience. Your conclusion may exercise one or all of the following functions: It may dispose your audience favor-ably toward you and your central thought. Remarks of a personal nature are often used in this type of conclusion. It may amplify the merits of your central thought. Additional exposition and illustrative material are often used. It may arouse your audience to heights of emotion, feeling, or deep concern, by exhorting and exciting them to action. Or it may simply recapitulate or summarize the important points used in the development of your central thought.

In preparing your conclusion you should beware of taking more time than necessary to conclude; introducing new ideas or points; trying to "make amends" for an inadequate development of your central thought; concluding by referring to the last point of your speech only; leaving your speech unended, leaving your audience un-certain; failing to unify your speech by diffusing attention, rather than focusing it on your central thought and its sub-points; and you should beware of being anticlimactic, letting your audience down suddenly.

13   Use of language

Thought units and sentences. Language is the basic factor in communication. To be communicative is to be understood. The degree to which the audience understands your thought is dependent, initially, upon the words you use and their arrangement into thought units. The thoughts of a speaker become clear as they are translated into words in meaningful combinations. Hence, adequacy in the use of language is based upon the arrangement of words in sentences.

You should construct your sentences carefully so that each idea is received by your audience as you intend it to be received. Construct your sentences so as to give your audience the complete and exact idea in an emphatic way. Use periodic sentences in which the important idea comes at the end. They provide opportunities for vocal emphasis and create suspense. Whenever it is possible, the words, phrases, or clauses that make up your sentence should be arranged climactically. When possible, use balanced sentences, in which similar or opposite ideas are "set off" one against another. Secure emphasis by separating an especially important idea from others, by placing it in a sentence by itself. Do not place an important idea in a subordinate clause.

Vary the construction of your sentences by using declarative, imperative, and interrogative sentences. Use the rhetorical question, in which the answer is implied, with your audience supplying it mentally if not actually. Use the direct question, the answer to which must be introduced by you.

Use variety in the length and complexity of your sentences. Use short sentences more frequently than long. Too many consecutive short sentences, however, make for a broken, choppy effect. Use simply constructed sentences more frequently than compound or complex. Too many simple sentences, however, may be offensive to some types of audiences.

You should always use acceptable grammar in the formation of your sentences. Acceptable grammar is that used by the majority of educated people. You should try to avoid certain errors of sentence structure, such as incomplete sentences—fragments; stringy sentences —sentences which need to be broken up into smaller units; choppy sentences—short sentences which need to be combined. You should avoid excessive coordination of sentences. Do not string thought units together with "and," "for," "because," "but." Eliminate these connectives. You should avoid long and involved sentences.

You should also avoid unusual sequence, order, and arrangement in sentence structure. You should avoid using verbs which do not agree with the subject—"They was (were) going home." Avoid using the incorrect verb form in relation to the tense (past, present, future)— "The mail has came" (come). Avoid using incorrect sequence of tenses—"I planned to have stopped" (to stop). Avoid using pronouns incorrectly—"It is him" (he). Avoid using incorrect contractions— "He don't" (doesn't). Avoid using adjectives for adverbs—"He did good (well) as an athlete." Avoid mixed constructions—"I am not going nowhere" (I am not going anywhere), "They are as following:" (They are as follows:).

Vocabulary. The more skillfully your words are selected the clearer the translation of your thought is likely to be. You should choose words for the expression of your ideas which are instantly intelligible to your audience to insure comprehension and prevent misunderstanding. Choose words with specific and exact meanings to insure correct and clear understanding by your listeners. Specific words stimulate the listener's imagination to a full realization of your meaning more quickly than general and abstract words do.

You should choose vivid, colorful words, in stating your thought, which will instantly stimulate the imagination of your audience, and aid them to visualize your idea in its complete detail. You should choose a variety of words. Avoid using the same word over and over again. Do not appear to have a limited and narrow vocabulary. You should feel free to use personal pronouns (I, you, we), thus placing yourself in a more personal, direct relationship with your audience.

You should avoid annoying your audience by your word choice. For example, you should avoid unfamiliar words. You should not use words and phrases that exaggerate your ideas in an unwarranted manner, such as "absolutely," "beyond a shadow of a doubt." You should avoid using common, hackneyed, meaningless expressions— "that thing," "and everything else," "and something else," "and so forth," "what-you-may-call-it," "day in and day out," "wheels of time,"—lest you be dull, trite, not clear, and possibly misunderstood. You should avoid vulgarisms and slang in its pure state—"youse guys," "whiffed the apple," "The big pay-off," "have a ball," "crack a book." Be sure you know the meaning of the words you use. If you have any doubt, consult a dictionary. You should avoid using too many words and inserting needless words. Finally, you should avoid omission of words necessary to the complete expression of your idea.

14   Projection to the audience

The term projection to the audience refers to the process by which the speaker sends forth his thoughts and feelings to the listener. It involves the initiation by the speaker, through the use of his voice and bodily activity, of the sound and light waves which carry his meanings to that listener. Effectiveness in projection is dependent upon the degree with which these sound and light waves vibrate with the full meaning and vigor of the speaker's thought and feeling. To project well, your bodily mechanism must function as a dynamic whole.

Know your speech.   Be thoroughly prepared! You should know your material, know what it means and what its implications are. If you do, you will speak with spontaneity and abandon. You will not be troubled with having to think of what to say next. You cannot project well and be uncertain about the plan and content of your speech.

Your attitude is vital.   You should have a wholesome, positive, dynamic attitude that can be characterized as follows: (a) You should be confident of yourself and of your success. This is not egotism. (b) You should appear interested in your subject, your audience, and the task before you. Audiences like the confident, interested speaker. (c) You should strongly desire to stimulate the thinking and reactions of your audience. (d) You should be intent upon accomplishing the goal you have chosen for your speech and eager to share your thoughts and experiences with your listeners. (e) You should be active, full of life and vigor—not passive, inhibited or unwilling to "let yourself go." (f) You should be friendly, pleasant and courteous.

Communicate with energy and enthusiasm.   You should be communicative. Speak with "a lively sense of communication." That is, you should: Speak with (1) an eagerness that is exhilarating; (2) a natural enjoyment that is charming and catching; (3) an evident but spontaneous muscular energy that is enlivening; (4) a released inherent enthusiasm that is contagious; (5) a sincerity and earnestness that is unquestionably convincing; (6) a depth of belief that is persuasive; (7) an emphasis and force that is irresistible; (8) a warmth that is personal.

49

Amplified conversation. To be communicative, you must be conversational, but let your speaking manner be that of amplified conversation. In one sense, it should be loud conversation. Whatever constitutes polite conversation when amplified to fit the situation is the basis of communicativeness. Remember that when you make a speech, it is to a number of people as an audience. Hence, the conversational manner suited to the "drawing room" simply will not do on the public platform. You are warned therefore that you cannot project well and be too conversational, too quiet, too easy. Your speaking manner must be sufficiently intense to stimulate the listener's complete attention. This absorbed attention by the listener will facilitate his reception with their full intensity, scope, and content of the sound and light waves which you send forth as you speak.

Make it a point to talk to your audience, not at them. Speak each idea directly to them as if it were a personal matter. Look at them. Face them. Keep direct eye contact with them. Avoid a constant "looking-about" from side to side, to floor, to ceiling, to speaker's stand while you are speaking. Not only will this mannerism annoy the audience but you will lose their attention thereby.

Speak Up! Speak Up! Speak Up! This is the key to effective communication with an audience. It takes energy. It is characteristic of enthusiasm. It gets and holds attention. It is one of the first and most important speaking habits for you to acquire.

Interpret the "Inner, Deeper, Richer Meanings." You must interpret for your audience the "inner, deeper, richer meanings" of your thoughts and feelings. You must sufficiently exaggerate these meanings in order to: stimulate an understanding, appreciating attention from your audience; make the depth of your meanings completely and clearly apparent to your audience; stimulate the imagination of your audience to a full reaction to and appreciation of your thoughts and feelings; fix your meanings vividly in the minds of your listeners so that they may be recalled by them easily; and secure from your audience an empathic response in which they "get into the spirit" of the situation with you. You make them feel as you feel. You cause them to respond strongly, whole-heartedly and without restraint to your thoughts and feelings.

15 Control of bodily activity

Bodily action while speaking is a natural occurrence. It is not an artificial technique to be acquired, to be used only by flowery orators. It is an inherent skill that you yourself possess. Bodily action while speaking, both gross and refined, occurs as you project your thoughts and feelings to your listeners. It arises from those thoughts and feelings as well as from the reactions of your immediate audience.

Under normal conditions, in simple speaking situations where ordinary conversation occurs, bodily activity is natural in the act of speaking and is adequate. In public speaking situations, however, it must be kept under constant control and used objectively and purposefully. Briefly then, bodily activity occurs naturally during speech, but when speaking in public, it must be controlled.

Though bodily action is naturally involved in projection to the audience, its importance in speech making warrants its emphasis as a separate technique in the total process of stimulating an adequate audience response. Hence, control of bodily activity is treated here separately as an essential of speech making.

Importance of experience. Use bodily activity freely from the very beginning of your practice in speech making. Use it with abandon. Have little concern, for a time, about "how you look" or whether the action is appropriate—just use it. Lose all of your inhibitions and self-consciousness as soon as possible.

The first step is to release the bodily action that is natural for you and which because of lack of experience you hesitate to use. The second step is to learn to control that action and make it purposive. In other words, your first job is to become able to use your own natural gestures comfortably when you want to use them before an audience, rather than to be concerned about when, how, or how well you use them. You will discover that if you follow this advice you will receive very little criticism and that you will need very little instruction in bodily action. Suggestions from your speech teacher may be helpful to you, but they cannot substitute for extended experience in making gestures while making speeches.

It should be very clear to you that effective bodily action is more a product of wide and varied experience as a speaker than of specific instruction or drill.

The whole body. The human body is a whole. It functions as a whole. It functions best as a whole. Its nature and condition may not only influence but may actually determine its behavior continuously or at a given moment. For example, the type and extent of action used by men while speaking is quite different from that used by women. Men use more action, broader and more forceful action, usually, whereas women use less action, less vigorous and more refined action.

Bodily activity includes posture, movement, gesture, and facial expression. All are simultaneously related to the thought and feeling of the speaker at the moment. Each is dependent upon the other. Though they may be studied separately, they, nevertheless, must be considered as a whole.

Movements of the parts of the body—the arms, hands, legs, head, face, eyes—arise from, individuate out of, are a refinement of total or gross bodily movement. A program of individual training in control of bodily activity might best proceed, therefore, as follows: (1) development of appropriate posture; (2) control of gross bodily movement—walking, broad gesturing; (3) techniques of platform movement—controlling bodily weight, use of legs and feet; (4) techniques in the use of the arms and hands in stimulating the listener and the audience to respond most completely; (5) control of head movements; (6) control of facial expression; and (7) control of eye movements.

Control posture. You should have a good posture. The position of your body, standing or sitting, should allow your muscles to function normally and with ease. There is no posture suited to all speakers but you should be guided by the following: Your posture should be comfortable. The muscles of your body should not be stiff or tense while speaking. They should instead be comfortably relaxed. Your posture should aid you in looking your best. Good posture is the basis of poise. It is an important factor in the impression that you make on your audience. Your posture should facilitate a free and easy functioning of your breathing mechanism and facilitate free and easy bodily movements in walking about the platform and in gesturing.

Experiment with the following in developing your best possible platform speaking posture. (1) Stand tall! (2) Stand on both feet with your weight equally balanced between them. (3) Keep your legs straight but not stiff, your knees relaxed. (4) Keep your shoulder, back, and neck muscles relaxed—free from strain and tenseness. (5) Allow your arms and hands to hang naturally at your sides. (6) Have your head up, your chin in, no tenseness.

You should avoid the following: (1) Standing with too wide a base, your feet wide apart. (2) Throwing your weight completely on one leg, thereby appearing unbalanced. (3) Leaning from your waist toward the audience. (4) Leaning backward with your weight on your heels. (5) Folding your arms across your chest. (6) Holding your arms tightly behind your back. (7) Placing your hands on your hips. (8) Keeping your hands in your pockets continuously.

Control bodily movement. You should control your bodily movement. You may wish to move about the platform. Such movement is probably wise if occasioned by the situation. You may desire to change your position, to relax, rest yourself, rest your audience, and increase the attention of your audience. You may desire to change your position to indicate transition of thought at the completion of the development of a portion of your speech. You may wish to move to secure a desired reaction from your audience, for example, move toward them to be more emphatic.

If you move, you should do it gracefully, but naturally and unnoticed, as such. You should step first with the leg toward the direction in which you are moving. Your weight before you move should be carried by the other leg. Make your movements decisive. Do not creep or side-step when you want to walk about the platform. Take natural, positive steps. Avoid unmotivated movement about the platform, movement which is not occasioned by the situation. Avoid mechanical movements which appear to be planned—so many steps one way, so many steps another. In case of doubt, stand still.

Control gestures. You may wish to use gestures. Effective gestures will aid you in projecting your ideas. Gestures help to get and hold attention. Since the arms and hands are the principal agents of gesture, you should note the following: (1) Your gestures should be in harmony with the thoughts and feelings that you express. They should vary in nature, duration, and intensity as your thoughts and feelings vary. (2) Your gestures should supplement adequately the vocal expression of your thoughts and feelings. They should not be overdone, neither should they be slighted. Each gesture should be a full gesture, completed and finished. Your hand and arm should not be just held up, then dropped. Let your gesture actually aid you in expressing your thought and feeling. (3) Begin your gesture "of the moment" as you begin speaking the thought to which it is related. Let it develop as that thought and the feeling associated with it develops. Let the gesture actually help to focus and hold the attention of the listener. This will aid you in being clear, being emphatic and in bringing the expression of your thought and feeling to a climax. (4) Your hand and arm gestures should be natural, graceful, free, and easy. They should be smooth, and rhythmical rather than abrupt and jerky. Each gesture should seem to flow into the next.

When your gestures are natural the whole arm is used and is used as a whole. That is, as the speaker uses his whole arm, the listener does not notice movements of the shoulder, elbow, wrist, or fingers, separately. Although the whole arm is used, it should not be completely extended in gesturing. Some restraint should always be used. The shoulder, elbow, wrist, and fingers are relaxed and flexible, not tense or stiff. Movements of the hand and arm proceed away from the center of the body. Hand and arm movements follow curved lines—the wrist leads the hand.

Practice the use of the basic types of "hands" in gesturing.

The pointing hand. The index finger is straight and strong; the rest of the hand is clenched somewhat tightly. This "hand" is used for directing attention to ideas as well as things. It is used to identify, to indicate location and to give a sense of direction. It is used to "point up" as well as to emphasize. This type of gesture is usually an active one, often vigorous. The finger and hand should not just be held up and then dropped. Both hands are not used simultaneously.

The giving hand. The "hand" is open, palm up. The fingers are fully extended. This "hand" is used in giving and receiving symbolically as well as actually. You give or take an idea as you give or take an object. This "hand" may accompany generalizations, appeals, interrogations, requests for consideration, attitudes of agreement, the making of admissions. It is sometimes used to suggest enclosing, encircling, encompassing. Both hands, right and left, are used in coordination, sometimes simultaneously. This "hand" is not usually a vigorous gesture, but is an active one.

The covering hand. Like the giving hand, this "hand" is open and the fingers fully extended, but the palm is down. The speaker may use this "hand" to indicate covering, quieting, subduing, pressing down, putting down, things beneath, encompassing, saying, "no—no." It is not usually a vigorous gesture. Both hands may be used coordinately and simultaneously.

The repelling hand. This "hand" is open, bent up at the wrist, fingers fully extended, palm toward the audience. It pushes away, repels, gets rid of, denies, forbids, nullifies, abrogates, cuts off or cuts down, abhors, protects, protests. It is an active gesture, vigorous at times with both hands used occasionally, sometimes simultaneously.

The clenched hand. This "hand" is a closed fist. It is the most vigorous of gestures expressing the strongest feelings. It pounds for emphasis, exhibits strength and force, indicates opposition, may symbolize courage, determination, anger, hatred, revenge. One or both hands are used. It is an active gesture.

You may use your hands in gesturing in ways other than described above but for the most part your "hands" will be of these specific types or variations, closely identified with one or more of them.

If you rehearse these types of "hands" appropriately, improved habits of gesturing can result. Your gestures may thus become less random and careless. Mannerisms, if you have them, will tend to be minimized or eliminated. With improved habits in the use of the basic types of "hands," your gestures will tend to be more objective and meaningful. You, as a person, will appear more coordinated, more poised, more refined.

The danger is that in rehearsing these "hands" improperly your gesturing habits may come to be mechanical. You avoid the mechanical by using a practice method which permits you to grow into the new habit instead of trying to acquire it all at once. In such a method, you practice first the gross or general form of the gesture.

Then, through criticism and further practice accordingly, you refine its use into natural behavior for you.

You should be aware of where you place your gestures. Ordinarily, you locate them appropriately and without forethought but it is well for you to be critical of how you locate them. Gestures are placed somewhat as follows.

Chest level and above. References to that which is tall, high, good; excellent, important, significant, worthwhile, noble. Gestures accompanying references to God, country, home, right, honor, duty, justice and the like.

Below waist level. References to that which is short, low, below, deep down; unimportant, insignificant, unworthy, bad, despicable, evil. Gestures accompanying reference to Satan, wickedness, wrong-doers, traitors, failure, condemnation, injustice, the grave, and so forth.

Between waist level and shoulder level. References to things normal, natural, regular. Gestures accompanying ideas neither high nor low in magnitude, quality, feeling, attitude.

Right or left of center. Reference to things at a distance, far away, remote, mystical, imaginary. Time, space, direction, geography are conditioning factors.

Center. References to that which is normal, natural, regular; to self, things personal, fundamental, primary, direct, to the point, near, close to home, real, practical, immediate.

Control head movements and facial expression. Head movements and facial expression are inherent in the act of speaking. They are spontaneous, natural, and adequate when the speaker is uninhibited. During speech making they may need to be controlled.

Head movements. Your head movements (front to back, side to side, rotating) in speech making, to be effective, must be used selectively and purposefully. They should not be random movements. They should be coordinated with your bodily movements and your hand and arm gestures. Your head movements can aid you in focusing attention, in expressing meaning, and in being emphatic. As in the case of your hand and arm gestures, your head movements must be timed just right.

Facial expression. Your facial expression can be a major factor in your effectiveness. If you do not have a mobile face, if you are habitually "dead pan," you should develop facial flexibility to the extent that it readily reflects in a natural way your thoughts and feelings and supplements strongly their vocal expression. To be effective, your facial expressions must be clearly and completely meaningful but unnoticed, as such. They must be purposeful, spontaneous, natural, and suited to your face and personality. They must not be random, meaningless, or out of harmony with what you are saying. Controlled facial expression helps to focus and hold the listener's attention. It adds depth, richness, and personal intensity and vitality to the vocal and bodily expression of your thought and feeling.

Although facial expression should be developed as a whole, you should give specific attention to the use of your eyes, your brows, and your lips. You should be certain that they are responsive to the mood, feeling, and emotional aspects of what you say as you say it. If not, practice to make them so. Also, be certain that you have no mannerisms of facial movement that will prevent them from responding freely to your thought and feeling as you experience it.

Sometimes it is a good idea to practice in front of a mirror, to study and experiment with your facial movements as you speak. Practice a smile now and then. Audiences like to look at speakers who seem to be pleased to be there, pleased to be speaking.

It is best to have your face as well-lighted as possible while you are speaking in order that your facial expressions can be easily seen by the audience as well as appropriately high-lighted to insure full effectiveness.

Adapt to the speaking situation. You should adapt your bodily activity to the speaking situation and control it accordingly. The more informal the situation, the more informal your behavior should be, but always within the requirements of good taste. The more formal the situation, the more formal your behavior should be—but avoid being too formal.

The kind of action needed will vary with your audience and the auditorium. Broad action is required for large mixed audiences, and more refined action for small, more select audiences. The amount of action needed will vary with your audience, its size, its physical condition (fatigued, fidgety, and so forth), its emotional state (sympathetic, prejudiced, and so forth), and your own emotional state. Use more action for large, or fatigued, or prejudiced audiences; use more action on festive occasions; but use less action for small, alert audiences, or for audiences gathered on solemn occasions. Usually, as tension increases, you use a greater amount of action and use it with more intensity. Use neither too much nor too little in any case. Keep yourself under control and use gestures selectively.

Common faults. You should avoid certain common faults in using bodily action: You should avoid unmotivated action—action that has no reason or purpose. Unmotivated action detracts from your effectiveness. Action should aid you in projection of thought and feeling or be omitted. You should, as a rule, avoid extreme, unusual action. Keep some reserve. You should avoid gesturing with the forearm only, and with the elbows close to the body. You should avoid indefinite, continuous movement and gesture, flipping your hands, pawing the air. Make your gestures specific, clean cut, and decisive, or omit them. You should avoid giving the appearance of gesturing at stated intervals, using a gesture because it is in a good place, and because you think you ought to use it there or because you rehearsed it there. You should avoid gesturing across your body. Use your right hand for gestures to the right, your left for gestures to the left.

You should avoid certain annoying mannerisms which may detract from your effectiveness: playing with your clothes—pockets, buttons, necklace, necktie, handkerchief; playing with objects—notecards, pencils, rings, watch chains, pens, keys, money, the chair, the speaker's stand, the desk; playing with your hands, your fingers; stumbling, shuffling your feet as you walk, bumping into furniture; looking out the window, at the ceiling, at the floor (semi-profile positions); pacing the floor. Don't appear restless by rising on your toes or heels continuously, or swaying back and forth. Do not use stereotyped gestures, and never use the same gestures over and over again.

16 Rhythm

Rhythm in speechmaking refers to the flow of the speaker's thought and language through vocal presentation. A speaker who is superior in *Rhythm* speaks fluently, smoothly, effortlessly; there is a "forward-moving" continuity in his thought and language. At the other extreme is the one who speaks with effort and regardless of how hard he tries is unable to make his speech mechanism function with a "forward-moving" continuity; the necessary timing in the integration of its parts is abnormally irregular.

Inadequacies. Listeners become aware of and are disturbed by the following inadequacies: Jerky, irregular speaking characterized by the repetition of sounds, syllables, words and even whole phrases; unusual pauses and hesitation inappropriate as to place, frequency and length of occurrence; vocalizing of pauses in which the sound "uh-uh-uh" or "ah-ah-ah" occurs. During hesitations "uh" or "ah" is sometimes added to words such as "he-uh," "they-uh," "well-uh," "and-uh," "for-uh"; voice patterns of pitch, intensity and rate in which identical voice inflections are repeated regardless of the thought being formulated; sudden utterance of phrases, words, syllables, or sounds which are unnatural and inappropriate at the moment.

If your speaking is characterized by any of these inadequacies, your effectiveness cannot help but be noticeably impaired. Your awareness of them is necessary for the most rapid improvement. It is important to recognize that you can improve the effect of your speaking by making it more fluent.

What to avoid. Improve the rhythm of your speaking, aid its "forward-moving" flow by learning to avoid certain common manifestations of poor rhythm: (1) Avoid speaking more slowly or rapidly than is normal for you. (2) Avoid sudden and unwarranted changes in your rate of speaking and the intensity and pitch of your voice. (3) Avoid using more intensity on the first syllable of a word or the first word of a phrase or sentence than on the remainder, unless necessary. (4) Avoid starting or ending all words, phrases, sentences at the same pitch level. (5) Avoid consistent repetition of the same variation of pitch, intensity, and rate of speaking; and the continuous use of the same inflections regardless of meaning. An example of the continuous use of the same voice inflections is often called "sing-song" rhythm. (6) Avoid adding the sound "uh" on the end of words, such as "and-uh," "well-uh." (7) Avoid vocalizing during pauses, for example saying "uh-uh-uh" or "ah-ah-ah" while you are trying to find the right word or formulate the next thought unit.

Breathing important. Check the effectiveness of your breathing while speaking. You should satisfy each of the following requirements. If you are unable to do so, you should practice until you can. These breathing skills are not only vital to fluency in speechmaking but they are also basic to adequacy in the fundamental processes of phonation and articulation, as well.

(1) You should be able to fill your lungs adequately either quickly or slowly. (2) You should be able to fill your lungs adequately without fatigue. (3) You should be able to exhale quickly or slowly as necessary. (4) You should be able to suspend and resume inspiration and expiration at will. (5) You should be able to sustain sounds or speak for a time on an ordinary breath. (6) You should be able to inhale quietly, noiselessly, as often as necessary. (7) You should be able to maintain a reserve supply of breath. (8) You should be able to breathe naturally without the awareness of the audience. Breathe without gasping. (9) You should be able to breathe without interfering with the muscular processes operating in the formation of sound.

Knowledge and preparation vital. You cannot speak fluently on a subject that you know little or nothing about. Neither can you speak fluently when your speech is inadequately prepared. You must choose subjects about which you have intimate knowledge, which are in the realm of your experience, and with which you feel "at home." Your subjects should be of the kind that you strongly desire to talk about, subjects that you will enjoy sharing with your listeners.

You must be sure of what you are going to say and how you are going to say it. You must carefully, thoroughly prepare each speech. You must be completely familiar with your material, its organization, and how you are going to develop each thought. You should not be "at-a-loss" as to what comes next. You must have thought about your speech, worked over it, lived with it long enough to know it well.

THE ESSENTIAL SKILLS OF SPEECH MAKING

Develop speaking readiness. Readiness to speak at one's best, regardless of the situation, requires a natural self-control of the functioning of the total bodily mechanism. This control makes for constancy and steadiness in the functioning of the speech mechanism. A constant and steady functioning of the speech mechanism makes for speaking that is fluent and effortless, and which seems to flow forward with a spontaneous easy-to-listen-to movement. Such speaking rates high in *Rhythm*.

It should be pointed out that the greatest deterrents to speaking readiness are emotional instability, excitement, nervousness, tenseness, stagefright. All cause your bodily and speech mechanism to function abnormally and upset its normal rhythm.

We indicated above that you will be more fluent in speech making if you avoid the more obvious characteristics of poor rhythm; if you have or develop good habits of breathing while speaking; if you speak on subjects within the range of your own personal experience; and if you are always thoroughly prepared. These immediate approaches to improvement in rhythm should be accompanied by a goal of longer range—speaking readiness as defined above.

To acquire this speaking readiness with its spontaneous, natural, forward-moving flow of utterance, be guided by the following:

Be relaxed, composed, confident, poised. Learn to keep your body relaxed, your feelings composed, your attitude confident during speech making. Each begins with a positive mental attitude which causes you to behave accordingly. Get started well when making a speech by thinking about what you have to say, immediately before you are called upon and while you are speaking, rather than worrying about yourself, how you will do, how you are doing. You should say the first sentence over to yourself several times immediately before you are introduced, in order to have it clearly in mind and hence, get off to a good start.

Take your time while you are speaking. Pause when necessary to visualize and formulate your next thought. Maintain an outward appearance of ease and relaxation.

Speak often. Take every opportunity to practice speaking to others. As a result, you will increase your facility for speaking through experience. Speak to all kinds of audiences in all kinds of situations.

Also attend social gatherings as often as possible and participate actively as a conversationalist. Speak impromptu; speak from prepared notes; read aloud at sight as well as from familiar materials; recite poetry and prose from memory. If you do not have real audiences to practice on sufficiently, speak to imaginary ones.

Hear good speakers. Take every opportunity possible to hear accomplished professional speakers. Keep yourself relaxed while you listen and put yourself in accord with the spontaneously fluent "forward-moving flow" of the speakers' thought and language. The influence on your speech will be indirect and subtle but nevertheless can be very marked.

Broaden your vocabulary. With more words at the "tip of your tongue," greater fluency is not only possible but probable.

17   Pronunciation

Characteristics. Pronunciation refers to the way sounds, syllables, and words are spoken in continuous speech. For your pronunciation to be acceptable, your spoken words should be pronounced as a majority of the respected people who hear you would pronounce them themselves. For your pronunciation to be superior, it should be free of provincialisms and sub-standard regionalisms, as well.

You should keep in mind that the section of the country makes a difference in the way some words are pronounced. Students of pronunciation have pointed out that in general there are three principal types of pronunciation in the United States—Eastern, Southern, and General American. By far, they say, the largest number of us are accustomed to General American pronunciations.

Some words have more than one acceptable pronunciation, though one may be preferable. Pronunciations may change with time, even from generation to generation. Uncommon, unusual, unfamiliar pronunciations must be avoided wherever you speak. In case of doubt, you should find out what pronunciations are recommended by consulting recent standard dictionaries. Learn to use these pronunciations regularly.

Acceptable pronunciation. Technically, to meet the qualifications of acceptable pronunciation, the speaker must choose the proper sounds, combine them appropriately into syllables and words, speak the sounds and syllables correctly and accurately, and give each syllable within the word its proper stress. Thus, for your pronunciation to be acceptable it must conform to the following specific qualifications.

Your speech sounds should be formed correctly and accurately. Inaccurate, careless, or slovenly formation of the speech sounds is responsible for most inadequate pronunciations. The correct speech sounds should be used in their proper place and order. For example, avoid the use of incorrect vowels—[gɪt] (get), [dʒɪst] (just). Avoid the use of incorrect consonants—[əsɛpt] (accept), [wɪtʃ] (which), [lɪbərdɪ] (liberty), [lɛnθ] (length). Avoid the addition of sounds—[draʊndɛd] (drowned), [ɪlənɔɪz] (Illinois), [ətæktɛd] (attacked), [lɔr] (law). Avoid the insertion of sounds—[ondlɪ] (only), [stəstɪstɪks] (statistics), [æθəlɛtɪk] (athletic). Avoid the transposition of sounds—[pɪrdɪ] (pretty), [prɛspɪreɪʃən] (perspiration). Avoid omitting necessary sounds—[gʌvərmənt] (government), [fɛbjuɛrɪ] (February), [dʒɛnlmən] (gentlemen).

Each word should be spoken with its proper accent or proper syllabic stress. For example, avoid overstressing unstressed syllables—['diːpɑrtmənt] (depart'ment), ['diːtrɔɪt] (Detroit'). Avoid misplacing accent or stress—[θi'eɪtr] (theatre), [supɪr'fluəs] (superfluous), ['polɪs] (police').

Obsolete, local, colloquial, vulgar, dialect pronunciations should not be used except to produce desired effects.

Adapt your pronunciation. You should pronounce your words more slowly, forming the syllables and consonants more precisely when speaking to audiences in large auditoriums; when speaking in auditoriums where the hearing conditions are uncertain; when speaking in noisy situations; and when your thought is especially significant and you wish to draw attention to it.

Use of dialects. When using dialects in story telling, your pronunciations should conform to the character types, the era and locality in which they lived or from whence they came. It is better to suggest dialect pronunciations than to reproduce them exactly. If

the dialect is spoken too exactly, the audience may not be able to understand what you say.

18 Voice control

Voice control, a special skill. Voice, like bodily activity, is inherent in the projection to the listener of the speaker's thought and feeling. Effective speakers rate high in *Projection to the Audience*. The most effective speakers also rate high in *Voice Control*.

When you speak spontaneously in every day situations, your voice tends to express your thoughts and feelings adequately. However, when you are making a speech to an audience, you are most effective when your voice "points-up" for the listener, in more than just a casual way, the "inner, deeper, richer meanings" of your thoughts and feelings. This pointing-up requires an objective and conscious control of your voice—its pitch, intensity, duration, and quality. Through effective *Voice Control*, you gain and hold your listener's attention more readily, you make your meanings clearer and sharper, you give them greater depth, making your meanings more vivid and stimulating to the listener. Of course, this conscious and objective control of your voice, to be effective, cannot be obvious or mechanical. It should seem habitual and natural.

Development of voice control. Effectiveness in *Voice Control* is developed through experience in speaking and reading aloud, voice training, and persistent directed practice. This training and practice, to be of value, must be in terms of specific voice skills needed in speech making.

Experience in speaking. Through experience in speech making and reading aloud, you become aware of the need for *Voice Control*. You learn what it does and what it can do for you in enriching your speaking effectiveness. You become especially alert to the nature of audience attention and reactions to voice changes and inflections.

Voice training. You must learn to recognize variations in your own voice—its pitch, intensity, duration, and quality. Your ear should

detect subtle as well as broad changes and inflections. Ear training is the first step in the development of voice control skills.

Experiment with the functioning of your vocal mechanism. Become aware of the kinds of sounds, tones and noises that it will produce. Produce these various kinds again and again until your mind and ear and vocal mechanism are so coordinated that when a specific sound or tone or noise is wanted the mechanism adjusts to produce it automatically.

Four basic types of experiments are especially helpful in developing *Voice Control* in speech making:

1. Experimentation with pitch level, pitch range and pitch inflection. Involved are adjustments within the larynx, principally of the vocal cords. Proper and sufficient experimentation results in clearer, more exact, more pointed, more subtle expression of the nature, the depth, the intricacy of your thought and feeling. This fineness of expression, made possible by controlled pitch modulations, results in easier, more attentive listening. The opposite is the result of inadequate control of pitch.

2. Experimentation with the size and shape of the mouth, throat, and nasal cavities and the openings to and from each. The soft palate, the tongue, the lips, the cheeks, the lower jaw, all are involved in one way or another in *Voice Control* affecting especially voice quality and intensity. The quality of your voice can become nasal, denasal, muffled, metallic, harsh, hoarse-husky, breathy, or infantile, as well as clear and pleasant according to the way you adjust the size and shape of the throat and nasal cavities and the openings to and from each. You will amaze yourself at what you can do with your voice in producing various types of voice quality. If you have a weak voice, proper adjustment of these cavities may help to make it stronger.

3. Experimentation with breath pressure in voice production. Your experimentation should result in: (a) Precision in the initiation of the necessary breath pressure to start the production of vocal tones of the required strength or intensity; (b) Precision in stopping vocal tones through discontinuing breath pressure; (c) Ease in maintaining steady breath pressure, weak or strong, in the production of vocal

tones for long or short periods as necessary; (d) The ability to increase or decrease the intensity of a tone during its production.

4. Experimentation with the duration of the tones of your voice. Your experimenting should develop your ability to: (a) Hold constant the size and shape of the cavities and their openings as long as necessary to produce vocal tones of the required duration, intensity and quality; (b) Hold constant the necessary breath pressure in relation to the adjustment of the cavities and their openings to produce vocal tones of the required duration, intensity and quality; (c) Change quickly or slowly the size and shape of the cavities and their openings and the required, related breath pressures to produce easily but accurately the variations in duration, intensity and quality of tone which are required to express the "inner, deeper, richer meanings" of the speaker's thought.

Voice control skills. Experimentation with your voice should lead to your acquiring certain skills: (1) The use of your total pitch range; (2) Ability to vary pitch within syllables, sounds, and words; (3) Ability to use rising and falling inflexions; (4) Ability to use your total range of intensity; (5) to vary intensity within sounds, words, and syllables; (6) to build up intensity—or diminish it; (7) to use longer or shorter duration of sound on words or syllables; (8) to vary the length of pauses at will; (9) to vary voice quality at will; (10) to reproduce rhythm patterns, inflectional changes and quality characteristics of people and dialects.

19   Audience response

The term audience response refers to the reaction of the audience individually and as a group to the speaker and the speech as a whole. For the response of the audience to be adequate, good will toward the speaker and general appreciation and understanding of his speech, its content and purpose, must be evidenced at its conclusion. The speech itself must be sufficiently stimulating to get attention quickly and hold that attention easily. The personal qualities of the speaker, as well as his thought and his manner of speaking, must have a pleasing effect on his listeners. The audience must be favorably disposed toward him.

Although speaking is studied in terms of its various fundamentals and essentials, the display of skill in each, independently, does not constitute effective speaking. Effective speaking is more than a combination of skills in choice of subject, choice of thought, choice of material, organization of material, use of language, projection to the audience, control of bodily activity, rhythm, pronunciation, and voice control. The speaker's skill in each of these essentials must unite, blend, combine into a nicely balanced whole—a total skill—to which each contributes, but in which none is noticed independently. And all must be in harmony with the speaker's personal characteristics, as well as with the factors present in the speaking situation.

Personal characteristics and behavior. Your personal characteristics must be attractive to the audience. They like to see you well groomed, wearing clothes chosen with good taste and not extreme or gaudy. They like your conduct on the platform to be in good taste, friendly, courteous, well mannered. They like to see you poised and dignified; exhibiting mastery of yourself and of the situation, showing confidence in your success, but not giving impressions of overconfidence, smugness, or conceit. Audiences like a speaker who is actively interested, energetic, and excitedly alive, but not tense and nervous; rather, relaxed and comfortable but not unconcerned or careless.

They want to hear and understand easily. They will, if your voice is pleasing and sufficiently loud, but not so loud as to call attention to itself. They want your pronunciation to be sufficiently correct to be acceptable and sufficiently distinct to be easily understood; your language, in addition to expressing your ideas clearly, in good taste; your bodily activity integrated with the thought and feeling as you express it and appropriate to the situation, not full of random movements which are distracting.

Audiences gain impressions from the moment you first appear until you retire. Hence, when you are seated on the platform, they prefer to see you sit straight, usually with legs uncrossed. When you are introduced by the chairman, rise, acknowledge the chairman with a nod and a smile perhaps, and proceed to the speaker's stand or near the center of the platform. Take a position before beginning to speak, pause, address the chairman and audience, and look directly at your audience as you speak your first sentence rather slowly, distinctly, and loudly enough to be heard easily. At the conclusion of your speech pause, take a step backward, walk to your seat, stop, face front, pause, sit down; do not fall or slump into your seat. Keep your eyes on the chairman and audience for a moment; then relax, but sit erect and be inconspicuous.

Adapting to changing conditions in the situation. To please your audience, you would do well to adapt your speech, as it develops, your style of presenting it, your behavior, and your manner to changing conditions in the situation. Your audience will respond with their attention in spite of distracting and disturbing factors which may occur. Sometimes their attention will lag. If it does, you must regain it. Sometimes you can do this by being more intense in projection. Sometimes it is necessary to introduce more and perhaps different but related illustrations, anecdotes, instances, and circumstances than you had originally planned to use. They must be especially interesting and stimulating to the immediate audience.

If the audience is uncomfortable, what can you do? If the ventilation of the room is bad, have doors and windows opened, if possible. If the audience appears to be suffering from the cold and windows are open, have them closed, if convenient. If the program has been long thus far and if the members of the audience seem tired and restless, some speakers have them rise, stretch, and relax, or they use some other method to accomplish the same result where the situation will permit it. If persons are standing in the room and seats are available, you might ask them to be seated before you begin your speech. Speak loudly enough so that all may hear easily. If the audience is extremely fatigued, listless, or uncomfortable, shorten your speech rather than continue at length under such circumstances.

Audiences are affected by disturbing factors. When things happen, your audience will respond favorably to you if you give evidence that you have complete control of the situation, that you are not irritated or upset. If a sudden humorous incident occurs, laugh with the audience. Allow them to respond to the incident fully, then turn the incident to your advantage if possible. If sudden noises, train whistles, passing fire engine, shouting, and the like occur, pause for a time, perhaps comment upon the disturbance, repeat your last sentence or two, then continue. If certain members of the audience "heckle" or interrupt you, respond with sincerity, good nature, and good taste, turning the incident to your advantage and thereby increase the sympathy of the audience toward you. If your audience evidences coldness, prejudice, or enmity toward you, win them, if possible, by a direct appeal for fair play and open-mindedness. Sometimes you may effectively use an indirect approach in which you present inherently interesting facts, anecdotes, or comments which are in themselves absorbing and stimulating and which capture attention.

If you make errors or incorrect statements, have trouble in getting under way or in saying what you mean, make the correction that should be made, perhaps beg the pardon of the audience, or make some other appropriate comment and proceed. Do not allow yourself to be disturbed if such things occur.

The audience will like it if you give the impression that what you do and the way you do it arises naturally out of the situation, your idea, your feelings, and their reactions.

The speech must be well received. In order to be rated superior in *Audience Response*, your speech must be well received by your audience. Your speech must be stimulating, interesting, enjoyable. The audience must desire to listen to you and be able to follow your presentation without too much effort. Your speech must provoke a feeling of general appreciation and understanding of your central thought. The audience must be pleased to have had the opportunity to hear you.

PART FOUR

The Essential Skills
of Reading Aloud

Introduction

There are two basic kinds of speaking: original and interpretative. In original speaking, the speaker presents his own ideas to an audience, whereas in interpretative speaking (reading aloud) the speaker presents the ideas of another, in the words of the author, and interprets their meaning as completely as possible or as may be necessary for the immediate audience. Although the ideas and words are those of another, the speaker's interpretation is his own; that is, it is based upon his own understanding of and his own experience in relation to what the author has written and the response he wishes to secure from his immediate audience. As in original speaking, the speaker, first, must get the attention and interest of the listener; second, he must hold that attention and interest throughout his presentation; third, he must make his and the author's thoughts and feelings clear so that the listener will understand and appreciate them; and fourth, through the manner of his presentation, he must fix these thoughts and feelings in the mind of the listener so that they may be recalled readily. And these demands on the reader hold wherever he may read, at a business meeting, at home, at church, or as a professional public performer.

Essentials of interpretative reading.   As in original speaking, there are basic essentials for study and practice in developing skill in reading aloud. These essentials, similar for the most part to those in original speaking, are: (1) *Choice of Material*, (2) *Arrangement of Material*, (3) *Projection of Thought*, (4) *Projection of Emotion*, (5) *Control of Bodily Activity*, (6) *Rhythm*, (7) *Pronunciation*, (8) *Voice Control*, and (9) *Audience Response*.

20   Choice of material

Material suited to the reader.   When you are considering selections of prose and poetry for reading aloud, ask yourself whether the selection in question is suited to you personally. Is it within the range of your own experience? Do you understand it? Can you visualize the author's meaning? Do you appreciate its "inner, deeper, richer meanings"? Can you interpret effectively for the audience the thoughts, moods, and emotions involved, as well as the characters, if any are included? Is it too difficult for you to read at this time? Do you have the time to rehearse it to read it well? Do you really want to read the selection, and will you enjoy doing it, if you can read it well? How much time will you have for the reading? What is your place on the program, if there is more than one reader?

It may be that you have done very little reading aloud before taking this course. In that event, be especially careful in selecting material that suits you. On the other hand, you may wish to experiment with several types of material—and there is no place better to do it than the classroom.

Material suited to the audience and the occasion.   Be certain that what you would like to read is suited to the audience and to the occasion. As in original speaking, you must analyze your probable audience in terms of its composition, age, common interests, intellectual and emotional levels, likes and dislikes, probable mood and behavior, occasion for the meeting, recent events, probable attitude toward you, and what will please them especially.

Again you might think of your classroom. Generally speaking, your classmates are much like you, with similar interests and backgrounds, though they are never identical, be sure of that. So, try things out on them, and check their response.

Long and short selections. In deciding upon suitable material in terms of your time limit, you may find it best to read a cutting from a long selection; or you may prefer to use two or more selections written by the same or different authors which, because of a common theme or mood, can appropriately be presented in one performance. But never choose a selection for the one reason that it is suited to the time limit.

21 Arrangement of material

Frequently the material you use will have to be adapted, rearranged, cut, and edited to best accomplish your purpose. Before reading the selection, you will usually find it necessary to do some or all of the following: give the title of the material; tell who wrote it; make selected, interesting comments about the author; give the reasons why the material is being read, or what the selection is supposed to illustrate; furnish background material to arouse interest in it; supply the time, place, and setting, if it is a story; clarify unusual expressions or characters which must be explained for the audience to understand their meanings fully.

If you use several selections you may build them around a theme which is made clear at the beginning. Arrange them, from first to last, in an order which develops the theme most satisfactorily, and as you progress, relate one selection to another and to the theme by appropriate transitional remarks.

Notes about introductory remarks. It is best to provide an appropriate introduction to the selection which you are going to read. It will give your audience an opportunity to become accustomed to your manner of speaking before you begin to read, as well as give you an opportunity to become acquainted with your audience and to adjust to the situation.

In your introduction, make necessary explanations about the selection to be read, such as reviewing its historical background, or supplying information about unusual circumstances or events of interest which are related to the reading. If you have chosen to make a cutting from a long selection, you will certainly include in the introduction a synopsis of the events that had preceded the particular episode you are about to read.

Frequently, by your comments at the beginning, you can point up the theme, the impression, the mood, or the universal appeal of the selection you are about to read. You might decide to talk about the author himself, that is, to give a brief biographical sketch, to discuss his personality, or to analyze his style of writing. In another instance, you might prefer to explain why the selection appeals to you, or the reasons why you decided to read it on this occasion.

In short, your introduction provides an appropriate setting for your reading, facilitates understanding and appreciation by the listeners, and disposes them favorably toward you and the reading that is to follow.

Notes about cutting material. Frequently you may desire to read a selection which is too long for the time allowed. Often such material can by proper cutting be made to fit the time, the audience, and the occasion. There are excellent poems, short stories, plays, and novels which, after being carefully cut, can become excellent reading material.

After carefully studying the selection, with a full understanding of the theme and its development, pencil out the unnecessary or nonessential parts. Undoubtedly, it will be necessary to add words or phrases or even sentences in various places to knit the story together, to bridge the gaps occasioned by your cutting, and to insure proper sequence and unity. After you have made the cutting, read the remaining selection aloud completely to determine what is needed further in the way of connecting words of your own. Write in these needed words or expressions and revise them until the selection reads easily and smoothly. Reread the selection aloud as a whole and continue the process of editing until the selection has unity and coherence and contains all the essential material but only that which is necessary to the full development of the author's theme. Be careful not to destroy or diminish the author's contribution. The final cutting should be a complete, finished unit in itself, not a series of excerpts which are obviously patched together.

We recommend the following steps and procedures:

1. Carefully read through the entire selection.

2. Identify and think through its principal points; condense these points into an outline for your guidance in making the cutting.

3. Now reread the entire selection, pencilling out unessential portions, especially long expositions or descriptions.

4. In some cases you will choose merely one incident from a longer selection. This episode must become a complete unit in itself; if it is, what precedes or follows it in the original will not be necessary to give it unity, after you have arranged your introduction.

5. In many instances, you may find that you are able to omit entire pages, chapters, or incidents. You will retain coherence by weaving in a few transitional sentences of your own to carry the story along when parts have been omitted. Occasionally it may be necessary to write in a few sentences, for a character in the story to speak in words consistent with his characterization.

6. Next, study the dialogue with a view to omitting any unnecessary passages. Most of the time you will find that you can omit the "he said," or "she answered" explanations of the author. You can make the characters identifiable through vocal change or head position.

7. If there are many characters, delete those who are unimportant or unnecessary in developing the story, scene, or incident. Occasionally, it may be necessary to reassign speeches originally intended for another person, and perhaps to rephrase them somewhat. If you have a scene in which two people speak, do not hesitate to combine two or three short speeches of a single character into one longer speech, omitting the interrupting comments of the second character.

The cutting of plays. In the cutting of plays the same general rules apply. But remember to give the setting, the time, the place, and the circumstances and to describe the characters. The playwright frequently supplies you with the proper words with which to "set" each scene and act.

In cutting a play, strive to retain theatrical expressions, for example, "As the scene opens, there is a light knock at the door. Barrie's voice is heard calling Susan, his wife."

You might end a scene in some such way as this, "Barrie lets the roses fall slowly at Susan's feet. She looks at him with untold wonder as the curtain falls on Act One."

For years, the late Burns Mantle, and other recorders of the activity of the American theatre have prepared shortened versions of the best plays of the year. Mantle carefully deleted portions of the script and added comments of his own, so that in perhaps twenty-five or thirty pages a faithful representation of the play was presented. Your problem is much the same, except that where he presented the entire play, which would take nearly an hour to read, you will present only a scene or at the most one act.

Cutting the novel. The cutting of a novel offers a few special problems, the foremost of which is the retention of unity and plot sequence. Constantly keep in mind the development of the theme or thesis on which the novel is based.

Other suggestions previously made apply definitely to the novel, such as the elimination of unnecessary characters, the deletion of long, expository and descriptive passages, and the rewriting of some narration into dialogue. If you choose to omit whole passages and concentrate on one major episode (which is easier than cutting a whole novel), you will need to be extremely careful in working out your introduction to the selection so that the audience may be properly prepared for what is to follow.

Cutting orations or speeches. Review the previous general suggestions on cutting. In cutting the oration or speech, you have a choice between two methods: you may retain the original as a whole and omit those portions which are not absolutely essential to the development of the central idea; on the other hand, you may decide to take only a portion, perhaps only one major point in the oration, and present it in its entirety. The length and nature of the oration or speech itself will frequently help to determine your choice of method.

22   Projection of thought

Know your selection.   When you speak your own thoughts, they have meaning to you and you speak them meaningfully. When you read aloud, you must understand and appreciate the thoughts of the author in order to read them meaningfully.

To fully understand what you are reading, you must know and appreciate the theme of the selection as a whole and its essential background factors. You must know the meaning of each paragraph, sentence, and phrase, and its significance in the development of the theme; the setting and its implications in the development of the theme and the action involved. You must know the characters included, their distinguishing characteristics, and their place and importance in the development of the theme. And you should know important facts about the author and the special circumstances surrounding the writing of the selection.

In other words, if the reader is to project effectively to his listeners the "inner, deeper, richer meanings" of what he is reading, he must first be fully aware of these meanings. He must understand them so completely that he speaks them as if he had originated them.

Use basic speech skills.   The effective reader evidences a thorough understanding of his material as he reads by proper phrasing of the words and the use of pauses and emphasis. Voice changes in pitch, intensity, duration, and quality, are in harmony with the thought being expressed and aid its expression.

Phrasing, pausing, emphasis.   By *phrasing* we mean the grouping of the words in a sentence into subsidiary groups or thought units, according to the thought being communicated, through the use of *pauses*, short and long. The pauses may or may not coincide with the grammatical punctuation within the sentence. However, the words must be appropriately grouped, for entire meanings can be changed by careless phrasing. The length of each pause will vary with the effect desired. Frequently, a pause will give emphasis to a particular word or group of words. If you pause just before the important word, you direct attention to what follows—you "point it up." Comedians frequently use this device, pausing just before the key word of the phrase and again after it to give the audience time to chuckle or laugh. Whole phrases or words within phrases which carry the more significant, special, key meanings sometimes need more accent, stress, or force than others in order that they may be *emphasized* and brought especially to the listener's attention. You must carefully determine what words or phrases should be given this special emphasis, since misplaced emphasis may distort the author's meaning.

Develop voice flexibility. Speakers who have flexible voices project thought more effectively while reading aloud than do those whose voices are less flexible. A flexible voice is able to respond more readily to variations and subtleties in the author's thoughts. You should practice constantly to develop a flexible voice capable of making fine as well as broad changes in pitch, intensity, and duration in order that you may project the meanings of the author's thought completely. Generally speaking, the more flexible your voice, the more effective you will be in projection of thought.

Develop bodily control. Selected bodily action can enrich the reader's expression of the author's thought. Work to develop control of your bodily activity in order to improve your effectiveness in projection of thought while reading aloud.

Projection of thought basic to projection of emotion. Although the projection of thought and the projection of emotion occur simultaneously, for purposes of study and practice they can be separated to advantage. Although we believe that most students need more instruction in projection of emotion than in projection of thought, let us emphasize that effectiveness in projection of thought is a basic essential.

23   Projection of emotion

An author uses words not only to express thoughts, but also to express moods, feelings, and emotions. Hence, to present the author's meanings effectively—the "inner, deeper, richer" ones—the reader must interpret not only the thoughts involved, but the moods, feelings, and emotions as well. To speak of moods, feelings, and emotions is to speak of one and the same thing, except that moods are perhaps more general than feelings; feelings tend to be more specific than moods, while emotions may be thought of as very intense feelings. For example, the mood of the story or the poem or the scene may be somber, heavy, or tragic, the feeling of the character involved may be initially one of utter dismay and confusion which, as it becomes more intense, may be recognized as fear.

Causes of inadequate projection of emotion. The projection of the emotional content of what the author has written is based upon how effectively the speaker projects the *thought* which the author is expressing. That the reader must pay especial attention to the projection of the emotional elements in a selection is emphasized by the fact that many who read aloud, even including many with training, usually project the thought of the selection adequately but do not, however, project with similar effectiveness the moods, feelings, and emotions which are inherent in or accompany the thought being expressed. When the emotional elements are not expressed satisfactorily, it may be that the reader may not sense, recognize, or identify the mood, feeling, or emotion involved. Or, he may not have experienced the respective mood, feeling, or emotion in reality or even imaginatively; hence his body or voice may have no basis for recreating its characteristics. In other words, the material he is reading may be too difficult for him. It may be beyond his emotional understanding.

The reader's body and voice may not be sufficiently flexible to create the characteristics of the mood, feeling, or emotion even though he senses it and appreciates it somewhat. Or, through lack of experience in public speaking, and interpretative reading especially, he may not be aware of what his body and voice can do in the expression of the emotional content of a selection or to what extent he must "let them go" in its expression. Or, it may be that he is inhibited in speaking, and especially in reading which requires emotional interpretation, because of poor adjustment in the speaking situation, and also because of attitudes on his part which make him react negatively to emotional expression—he "holds back" the expression of emotion rather than "giving out" as he speaks.

Characteristics of skill in projection of emotion. It is clear that when we are uninhibited and speak our own thoughts, we express the related moods, feelings, and emotions appropriately and well. But it is quite different for most of us when we read aloud to listeners the thoughts of another. To present effectively what an author has written, we must speak as if what we are reading is our very own composition. It is clear that the most difficult of all is the interpretation of the emotional elements. This needed skill in projection of emotion generally and in any given selection can be developed.

The characteristics of the reader skilled in projection of emotion, which clearly indicate the goals toward which the inexperienced reader must work, are as follows:

1. He identifies, or senses readily, the moods, feelings, and emotions involved in the material he plans to read or is reading.

2. He has an appreciation for and an understanding of moods, feelings, and emotions generally and knows their nature and characteristics as a basis for producing them as he speaks. He has gained this knowledge through observation, study, and his own emotional experiences, both real and imaginary.

3. He has a readiness to interpret moods, feelings, and emotions as he reads. This readiness has been acquired through uninhibited as well as controlled experiences in reading aloud all kinds and types of material. He approaches what he reads with an intense inner enthusiasm and vigor.

For the inexperienced reader, we recommend that he begin with very simple material, such as the simpler, somewhat raucous children's stories, increasing the complexity and difficulty of the material he reads as his skill in projection of emotion increases. The children's stories may be read at sight, at first, with complete abandon and freedom of expression, the moods, feelings, and emotions being expressed as the reader reacts to them at the moment and with much exaggeration. It is best to read many stories of all kinds, stories in verse and prose, stories that are real, fanciful, descriptive, expository, dramatic, humorous, ludicrous, glamorous, gentle, villainous, and so forth, rather than to practice a great deal on just one or two. Later, some favorites may be studied and rehearsed with profit.

4. He has developed a flexible body and voice which can create the

79

essential characteristics of the various moods, feelings, and emotions. This flexibility of body and voice can be attained best through first reading simple material with complete abandon and with exaggeration of bodily and vocal expression which is spontaneous as the speaker reads. More difficult material should follow as the student develops flexibility of body and voice; suggestion and criticism should be increased and be made more specific as rapidly as the student can benefit from it.

This "flexibility of body and voice" is acquired as part of the "readiness to interpret" described in point 3 above, but each may receive separate emphasis as necessary. Emphasis on one also may hasten the development of the other.

5. He knows when his body and voice are producing the necessary characteristics of the mood, feeling, or emotion to insure recognition by the audience and the response from them he desires. The reader not only knows the effect he wishes to produce in the listener, but he knows *how* to produce it and knows *when* he is producing it.

6. He has so thoroughly mastered, through study and practice, the interpretation of the author's thought and feeling, that, as he reads, his body and voice interpret from phrase to phrase instantaneously, naturally, and effortlessly what the author is saying without seeming to have studied and rehearsed that interpretation.

Learning to express a mood, feeling, or emotion. Occasionally, the reader finds it necessary to express a mood, feeling, or emotion that is not within his experience and, hence, is difficult for him to create. In such a case, we suggest that the reader attempt to induce the mood, feeling, or emotion within himself and then experiment with speaking the author's thoughts in his (the reader's) own words until his expression is convincing. Then, in the same emotional manner, he should speak these thoughts in the author's exact words and rehearse their expression until he can reproduce the author's emotional meanings at will. Although the speaker may not actually be experiencing the mood, feeling, or emotion that he is expressing, the listener responds appropriately to what the author is saying as if he were experiencing it.

Various methods are used to induce moods, feelings, or emotions within a reader. All of the following suggestions may be helpful to the student.

1. The reader relaxes his entire body and puts out of his mind all thoughts except those pertaining to what the author has written. He may sit or stand or be slowly moving about, as he wishes.

2. He tries to imagine, to see in his "mind's eye," the situation the author has described, the setting, the characters, and what is happening. He tries to sense through smell, taste, touch, sight, and hearing, as well as in his muscles, the nature of the surrounding atmosphere. In this imaginative condition, he may do one or a number of things to further induce within himself the appropriate emotional state.

    a. He may literally think himself into the predominant mood, feeling, or emotion he must express.

    b. He may talk himself into it.

    c. He may have someone talk him into it.

    d. He may surround himself with pictures of a similar situation portraying a similar atmosphere.

    e. He may read a story involving identical moods, feelings, or emotions, or he may have an experienced performer read such a story to him.

    f. He may listen to appropriate emotional music.

3. To aid this imaginative approach, he may assume the body posture and tensions which seem most characteristic of the mood, feeling, or emotion involved and actually express it in pantomime. These assumed bodily postures, tensions, and movements may help materially in providing the muscular basis for the vocal expression of the mood, feeling, or emotion.

4. As the mood, feeling, or emotion seems to take hold of him, he may first express what he feels through noises, cries, moans, sighs, sobs, gasps, ejaculations, and so forth, followed by expression in his own words, in the same emotional manner, of what the author has written, followed by expression of the author's emotional meanings in the author's exact words.

5. He should analyze and describe what he does as he expresses the mood, feeling, or emotion to make certain that his rendition

approaches reality, that it is consistent with human nature and human behavior.

6. He should repeat a number of times the emotional interpretation he has learned, using other materials in order to insure that his body and voice will have a readiness to respond appropriately when confronted with a similar mood, feeling, or emotion in his reading.

24   Control of bodily activity

Bodily activity normally accompanies the thoughts and feelings a speaker experiences while he is speaking. As the thoughts and feelings of the author are expressed by the interpretative reader, his over-all bodily movements, his arm and hand gestures, and his head movements and facial expressions may play an especially appropriate and important part in his interpretation.

Further, the amount and kind of bodily activity used by the interpretative reader will vary with the individual reader, his selection, the occasion, and the nature of his audience, just as in speech-making. Obviously, the bodily activity that a reader would use in presenting Hamlet's *Advice to the Players* would be greater in amount and of a type different from what he would use if he were reading a quiet lyric. Hence, the control of bodily activity while reading is most important.

It should be emphasized that the effective reader gives the impression of poise, naturalness, ease, and simplicity. It is clear, however, that the bodily action used in any selection should be carefully planned and rehearsed, but rehearsed sufficiently to become natural.

The basic principle of control of bodily activity in interpretative reading is that the reader suggests bodily tensions and actions rather than attempting to make them complete and real. He suggests the bodily movements of the characters he is presenting rather than attempting to act them out completely. For example, in reading of the desperate struggle of the climbers in James Ramsey Ullman's *The White Mountain*, the reader's movements would not actually be the same as those of the climbers, but would rather suggest the muscular tensions involved.

THE ESSENTIAL SKILLS OF READING ALOUD

Your teacher will observe your good and bad qualities with respect to control of bodily activity while reading and will be most concerned about whether your posture is good, whether you appear well poised, handle your book properly, have sufficient eye contact with your audience. He will be further concerned about whether your general bodily tensions and movements are appropriate, whether your specific hand and arm gestures are right and natural, your facial expressions are suitable, whether the actions of the characters you are presenting are satisfactorily suggested, and whether you have any distracting bodily mannerisms.

As far as *Control of Bodily Activity* is concerned, you will be instructed and criticized principally on these points.

Notes on handling a book or manuscript while reading aloud. Except in very informal situations, most interpretative readers stand rather than sit while reading. If a reading stand or lectern is available, place your book on it; both hands are thus left free. If necessary, because of your height and vision, and it is possible, adjust its height beforehand so that it will be comfortable for you. If you sit while reading, you may wish to place your book on a table of appropriate height. If you read from several sources, plan how and where you are going to place your books or papers on the reading stand or table before you read from them and as you are through with them.

If the reading stand or table cannot be adjusted to the proper height for you to be comfortable, hold your book. If you hold it, place the book in one hand, so that you will have the other free for gesturing and turning the pages. If the book is unusually large or heavy, you may need to hold it with both hands. Practice using it so that you can do so easily and so that it will not inhibit your bodily activity.

Sometimes you will read selections from different parts of a book, or you will have to cut the selection so that you need to skip many pages at a time. Some persons insert at the proper places small pieces of paper on which the page number is written, so that they know the order in which the parts follow each other; the difficulty here is that the paper slips may fall out of the book. Other readers use paper clips or rubber bands to advantage in marking the pages from which they wish to read. Some prefer typing a copy of the cutting and placing it in a small looseleaf notebook, rather than reading from the marked-up cutting. In typing the copy from which you will read, do it in double or triple space; experiment to find which method you like best.

Turn the pages quietly without attracting attention. Do not wet your finger before turning the page. As you turn the page, look ahead in order to be certain of what comes next so that there will be no break in your reading, and your performance will progress as smoothly as it would in the middle of a page.

Bodily activity and type of material. The bodily activity of the speaker arises from his ideas and feelings as he expresses them. The bodily activity used by the reader is directly related to the thought and emotional content of the material he is reading.

When he reads factual material for the sole purpose of presenting clearly the ideas of the writer, the bodily activity that he uses is natural and at a minimum. His posture, his general bodily attitude, his facial expressions, and his arm and hand gestures are his own; that is, they are as they would be if the ideas he is speaking were original with him at the moment.

Descriptive material may occasion more action which supplements and actually aids the reader in making the writer's ideas vivid. This action is natural also. But when, in order to read his material effectively, the reader must suggest the attitudes, feelings, emotions, and moods that the characters involved are experiencing, as well as their physical characteristics, he assumes postures, creates bodily tensions, magnifies facial expressions, uses selected head movements and arm and hand gestures as appropriate, all of which supplement his vocal expression of the author's thoughts.

What bodily activity to use. Where the words are insufficient for the reader to express the writer's full meaning, or where the reader's interpretation demands special emphasis, controlled bodily action should be used. But what action should be used, and how? It is not possible to say here, since the material, the characteristics of the reader, and the intonation, all must be considered. These questions can be answered only by saying that the reader must:

1. Develop a flexible, responsive bodily mechanism.

2. Understand and appreciate thoroughly the "inner, deeper, richer meanings" of his material.

3. Be observant of the behavior and reactions of people.

4. While rehearsing his reading, use his imagination to the full in experimenting with bodily action until he discovers what action best supplements the thoughts and feelings he is expressing.

5. Select the most suitable action and exaggerate it sufficiently to make certain of the listener's response to it.

25   Rhythm

There is rhythm in many things, for example, in the sound of the wind and the rain, marching feet, a dance, the tick of a clock, the song of a bird, the beat of a heart, the laughter of a child, the beat of a horse's hoofs, the roar of an engine, the breathing of a tired man, the chant of a crowd, the way a foreigner speaks, the way you speak naturally, and the way you speak as you express various feelings, moods, and emotions. The effective interpretative reader captures this beat, accent, and movement, and controls it as he expresses the writer's thought and feeling.

Nursery rhymes when read aloud have a rhythmic sound, each according to the way it is written. In fact, all writing when read aloud has a rhythm which arises from the thought of the author, from the action, mood, emotion, and feeling he is expressing, as well as from the style of writing. In some writings, the rhyme scheme (such as agreement in sounds at the ends of lines and within lines, word groupings, and repetitions) is so basic and so predominant that the reader finds it difficult to subordinate the rhythm to the thought as he reads. Ordinarily, the rhythm of the selection, as such, is secondary to the expression of the author's thought and feeling but arises from it.

In other words, the interpretative reader must sense the rhythm, the movement, of what he is reading—fast, slow, accented, smooth—arising out of its meaning, background, thought, and emotional content, whether description, narration, or dialogue. The thought, the mood, and the form of the writing all will help the reader to determine and control the rhythm of his expression. He must, however, avoid following the form of writing alone, lest the reading become patterned or singsong; the thought element must predominate, rather than the rhyme or the printed line. He must read the ideas according to their meaning as they are related to the mood and emotion being expressed, even ignoring punctuation if necessary.

26   Pronunciation

The interpretative reader must pay especial attention to his pronunciation. Since the language used is the author's rather than the speaker's, pronunciation problems may be present. The selection may include unfamiliar words the pronunciation of which must be checked in the dictionary. It may involve dialectal pronunciations the nature of which may require considerable study and practice for the reader to reproduce them. The style of writing may introduce pronunciation difficulties requiring concentrated practice. It is clear that one who reads aloud to any extent must develop a range of pronunciation skills to aid him in interpreting what the author has written.

To acquire the range of pronunciation skills, one must:

1. Make a habit of looking up the pronunciation of all unfamiliar words and practice their pronunciation sufficiently, singly and in the text, to insure natural pronunciation of them.

2. Train his ear to recognize pronunciation differences, such as omission, substitution, and distortion of sounds, differences in syllabification, accent, and inflection, and differences in style or manner of pronunciation, such as casual, pedantic, and the like.

3. Practice to reproduce variations in pronunciation characteristic of the various regions of the United States and the more common foreign pronunciations of English, such as Italian, Scandinavian, French, and so forth.

Effectiveness in pronunciation in interpretative reading is determined by:

1. Whether the reader can be understood both in his normal pronunciations and in his use of dialects. Too exact reproduction of a dialect may make it difficult or impossible for the listener to under-

stand what is said. It is best to suggest the flavor only of the dialect by reproducing its outstanding and identifying characteristics.

2. Whether the style of pronunciation or the dialect used is appropriate to the author's thought and feeling; whether it helps in its interpretation and is therefore convincing.

3. Whether the pronunciation is easy, effortless, fluent, and natural. The reader's pronunciation should not call attention to itself, but rather should seem to be inherent in his interpretation. It should be emphasized that lack of fluency and ease in pronunciation may spoil the effect of the reader's interpretation.

27   Voice control

Wide range of voice skills essential. The control of the voice is a major factor in the effectiveness of the interpretative reader. Through skill in its control he secures responses from his listeners that otherwise might not be attained. Although he may cause his whole self to vibrate with the thought and feeling he is expressing, the effect of his interpretation on his listeners will depend upon the degree with which his voice is controlled to stimulate them to a complete realization of all of the essential details of that thought and feeling. Hence, the interpretative reader must have a wide range of voice skills instantaneously at his command—skills in control of pitch, intensity, duration, and quality, individually and in combination. These skills, acquired consciously at first, will become habitual with practice.

Bad habits in voice control while reading. When performances in extemporaneous speaking and reading aloud by the same persons are compared, it has been observed that many of the reading performances are characterized by one or more of the following:

1. A higher pitch level.
2. A more rapid rate of speaking.
3. The reading tends to sound monotonous in that there is less variation in one or more of the attributes of voice, especially pitch, duration, and quality.

4. One or more vocal patterns, especially of pitch, intensity, and duration, are apparent.

When one (or more) of these characteristics appears, voice control is inadequate.

Steps in developing voice skills. To develop the necessary range of voice skills required for effective interpretative reading, the inadequacies listed above must be eliminated. Here are some recommended steps:

1. Learn to take your time while reading, avoiding what may be called reading too rapidly. Rapid reading is not conducive to effective interpretation, whereas a slower reading rate may make it possible.

2. Learn to read in your normal pitch range, which is more nearly that used when you are speaking extemporaneously at ease and with poise.

3. Break yourself of any habits you may have of reading in patterns regardless of the author's thought and feeling. Practice to acquire a wider range in the use of pitch, intensity, duration, and quality.

4. Strive through practice to secure greater skill in the variation of pitch, intensity, duration, and quality within words, syllables, and even in sounds, as well as in phrases and sentences.

Most students will find that successful practice in these steps tends to eliminate their bad habits in voice control while reading aloud, as well as to provide the basis for acquiring a wider range of voice skills and hence greater effectiveness in interpretative reading generally.

Voice control should be spontaneous. It should be understood that the listener should not be aware of your voice or your control of it. He should react to the thoughts and feelings of the author, not to your voice skills as such. But, nevertheless, it is your skill in controlling your vocal instrument, spontaneously and effortlessly, that is the primary factor in producing a spontaneous, absorbing response from the listener. It is to be expected that the finest actors are most skillful in the control of their voices.

28   Audience response

When an interpretative reader appears before any group of listeners, his purpose should be to stimulate and entertain them, rather than to display his artistic skill as a reader. He reads to them for their interest and enjoyment; they have not come to watch him perform. It is this basic purpose that determines what the reader reads and how he reads it.

The effective reader blends his skills in all of the essentials of reading aloud—*Choice of Material, Arrangement of Material, Projection of Thought, Projection of Emotion, Control of Bodily Activity, Rhythm, Pronunciation*, and *Voice Control*—into a total effect to which all contribute and to which the listeners respond. The test of effectiveness in interpretative reading, as in original speaking, is how the audience individually and collectively reacts to the speaker and to what he presents as a whole. Inadequacy or especial excellence in any one of the essentials may impair the reader's effectiveness; for example, material not within the range of experience of the listener, poor projection of emotion, or very precise pronunciation.

While he is reading, the reader should sense the nature of the attention of his listeners and observe their reactions. If their response is not satisfactory, he should, if possible, change his style of reading to improve their reaction to what he is presenting; for example, speak with more energy, more slowly, or more distinctively, or be more emotional, and the like. Although the reader is somewhat limited by his material, he can and must adapt and adjust what he does and the way he does it to factors within the situation, the audience, the kind of room or auditorium, the acoustic conditions, what happens as he continues, and so on, in order to improve the attention and response of his audience.

Reading recitals.   Occasionally audiences gather to hear students as well as professional readers present what are frequently called "reading recitals." In such situations, the response of the audience may be influenced by a number of things that the reader may control.

The reader should give consideration to the way the platform is "set," the lighting, his introduction (if there is a chairman), the seating of late comers while he is reading, and so forth.

He must give special consideration to his dress and appearance. In general, simplicity in dress is best, that which is in keeping with what constitutes good grooming in any social situation. Your clothing should be in good taste for you in the specific situation from the standpoints of color, design, and fit. Your dress should not be extreme or gaudy and should never call attention to itself.

Whether formal or informal attire—a dinner dress, a tuxedo, or street clothes—is to be worn will be determined by the customs of the community and the nature of the occasion. Where several readers appear on the same program, it should be understood that all are to dress formally or informally—as agreed upon.

New clothes and new shoes should be worn during rehearsals so that the reader may acquire ease and comfort in wearing them. If you are uncomfortable in your clothes, your audience will suffer with you.

Ordinarily, no special make-up is necessary; if the lighting requires it, it may be worn, but it should not be extreme. Girls should not experiment with a new or unfamiliar arrangement of their hair.

In general, jewelry should not be worn, especially bright, reflecting ornaments and the dangling variety of bracelets and earrings.

PART FIVE

Assignments

29   Speech inventory assignments

There are six assignments in this section. Your instructor will decide how many he wishes to use with your class. Some instructors may use them all. Others may feel that two or three are sufficient to show "where you are now" in your progress toward becoming an effective speaker.

Assignment 1

Please write down a good bit of information about yourself, according to the following suggestions. Prepare to hand the paper in for your instructor to see. Then plan to stop at his office to discuss your background with him. Organize your material according to these eight items:

1. PERSONAL. Include your name, age, birthplace, present address, phone number. How is your health? Have you ever had any serious illness?

2. EDUCATION. Include grade school, high school, college, present status in school, major interests in school.

3. FAMILY. How many in your family? Are your parents living? Where were your father and mother born? What language was spoken in their home? What language do they speak now? Who

taught you to speak? With whom do you live now? What is the occupation of your parents?

4. TRAVEL. In what towns and cities have you lived and at what ages? To what states and countries have you travelled? Are you able to speak any other language than English?

5. WORK. Have you worked part-time or full-time anywhere? Doing what? What do you want to make your life's work?

6. HOBBIES AND ACTIVITIES. What do you like to do in your leisure time? Name the magazines you read regularly. Name the last three books you have read. Do you take part in civic, fraternal, or church activities? What?

7. SPEAKING. Have you had opportunity to speak to groups within the past year? What was the occasion? Within the past five years? On what occasions? Have you had any previous courses in speech? Have you had private lessons in interpretation or dramatics? Do the members of your family do public speaking? How do you feel when you are asked to make a talk? Have you ever been in a play or speech contest?

8. SELF-EVALUATION. Think of several people whom you consider good speakers. In what characteristics are you like them? i.e., what assets do you have that might make you a good speaker? Do you have some characteristics that might hinder your becoming a good speaker—some liabilities, so to speak?

Assignment 2

Now, let us give you a chance to make a short speech in order to estimate your adequacy in the fundamental processes. Select one statement from among those listed below, to be used as the subject of your speech. You may explain it or interpret the meaning of the statement, or you may discuss its significance. Illustrate it with examples from your own experience, if possible. Do not write out this little talk. You probably won't even need an outline. Plan your talk by thinking about it. Do not memorize it word for word. Plan to talk for not less than 2 nor more than 3 minutes. Present the talk extemporaneously and without notes when you are called on. Give your *Speech Handbook* to your instructor. He will evaluate your presentation by marking each of the four items in the appropriate

SPEECH INVENTORY NO. 2

The Basic Processes of Speech

(An individual diagnosis)

Student _____

Subject _____

ADJUSTMENT TO THE SPEAKING SITUATION: 7 6 5 4 3 2 1

Inadequacies: Ill at ease, unnatural, tense, inhibited, nervous, excited, frightened, hesitant, uncertain, chaotic, bodily mannerisms, unable to speak coherently, fluently, emphatically.

FORMULATION OF THOUGHT: 7 6 5 4 3 2 1

Inadequacies: *Successive thoughts* unrelated, interrupted, inconsistent; *Statements* ambiguous, obscure, inexact, incomplete, frequent grammatical errors; *Vocabulary* limited, inaccurate, colloquial, dull, inexpressive; *Pronunciation* noticeably incorrect, inaccurate.

ARTICULATION: 7 6 5 4 3 2 1

Inadequacies: Organic abnormality; jerky, uneven utterance, incorrect formation of some speech sounds; inaccurate formation of speech sounds; inactivity of the articulators, rapid rate of utterance; foreign accent.

PHONATION: 7 6 5 4 3 2 1

Inadequacies: Organic abnormality; *Pitch* too high, upward slide; falling inflection; *Intensity* too weak, too loud; *Duration*—tones held for too short a time; too long a time; *Quality*—improper balance or control of resonance, unpleasant, peculiar; voice lacks flexibility.

Comments:

7—Superior
6—Very Good
5—Good
4—Adequate
3—Poor
2—Very Poor
1—Inferior

_____   _____
Date   Evaluator

93

column. Most people are adequate in these four aspects. Accordingly, most of the scores will be "4." Some may be good ,"5." A few may be very good, "6." There may even be a student now and then who will be superior, "7." On the other hand, some may be poor, or very poor, or inferior, in which event your instructor will check the column for "3," "2," or "1." In that case he will underline the explanatory words which indicate in what way you are not adequate.

Each of the following statements is the last sentence of one of Aesop's fables.

The race is not always to the swift.
It is very foolish to be greedy.
Do not believe everything that you hear.
Pride goes before a fall.
Might makes right.
Learn from the misfortunes of others.
Friends in fine weather only are not worth much.
A kindness is never wasted.
If you try to please all you please none.
Self help is the best help.
Ability proves itself by deeds.
Misfortune is the test of true friendship.
Whatever you do, do with all your might.
There is nothing worth so much as liberty.
A possession is worth no more than the use we make of it.
Wicked deeds will not stay hid.
Do not count your chickens before they are hatched.
Take warning from the misfortunes of others.
An act of kindness is well repaid.
Be content with your lot.
Honesty is the best policy.
In unity is strength.
Act in haste and repent at leisure.
Look before you leap.
Do not grudge others what you cannot enjoy yourself.
Greatness has its penalties.
Take what you can get when you can get it.
One falsehood leads to another.
Stick to your trade.
However unfortunate we may think we are there is always someone worse off than ourselves.
Do not play tricks on your neighbors unless you can stand the same treatment yourself.

Be sure you can better your condition before you seek a change.
There's a time for work and time for play.
Deeds count, not boasting words.
Precious things are without value to those who cannot prize them.
You are judged by the company you keep.
It is easy to be brave when there is no danger.
Heaven helps those who help themselves.
Do not let anything turn you from your purpose.

Note: Some instructors have found that they can evaluate your adequacy in these basic processes of speech if you tell about some experience you have had. You and your instructor may decide to do this. Go ahead. It serves the same purpose. Don't talk too long.

Assignment 3

The third step in our inventory is designed to give us an idea of your present ability in the essential skills of speech making. To do this we ask you to make the best speech you possibly can to your classmates. You may speak on any subject you wish. You may give an informative speech, an argumentative speech, or an entertaining speech. You may talk about persons, places, things, events, experiences, opinions, or any other thing.

This speech should be three minutes in length, no more, no less. It is important for you to be able to stay within time limits. Remember that there are other speakers to be heard.

Plan your speech well. You should have several days to prepare after the assignment has been made. Begin early. Choose a subject for your speech that is worth talking about, that encompasses material worth listening to, and that arises out of a background with which you are familiar. Do not use a speech you have previously given.

Analyze the subject and carefully select the points you wish to present. Sort your material so that it is definitely related to your subject and the specific points you wish to develop. Arrange the material to secure unity, coherence, and emphasis.

Write out a detailed outline of the speech. This outline is to be handed to your instructor together with your *Handbook*, before you go to the platform to speak. Study the outline so that you are thoroughly familiar with the order in which you wish to present your material. Do not memorize the speech word for word. Practice the speech aloud many times.

ASSIGNMENTS

When you are called upon, go to the platform and speak loudly enough to be heard, speak clearly and distinctly, speak to secure the attention and interest of the audience, speak with vigor and enthusiasm.

This speech is important; it is essential that you be at your best. You may not speak as well or you may speak more effectively than others. In either case be sure that this performance is the best you can do.

SPEECH INVENTORY NO. 3

Achievement in Speech Making

Student _____

Subject: _____

Comments:

Choice of Subject	7	6	5	4	3	2	1
Choice of Thought	7	6	5	4	3	2	1
Choice of Material	7	6	5	4	3	2	1
Organization of Material	7	6	5	4	3	2	1
Use of Language	7	6	5	4	3	2	1
Projection to the Audience	7	6	5	4	3	2	1
Control of Bodily Activity	7	6	5	4	3	2	1
Rhythm	7	6	5	4	3	2	1
Pronunciation	7	6	5	4	3	2	1
Voice Control	7	6	5	4	3	2	1
Audience Response	7	6	5	4	3	2	1

Total score _____

7—Superior
6—Very Good
5—Good
4—Adequate
3—Poor
2—Very Poor
1—Inferior

Distribution
Above 60—Excellent
50 to 60—Good
39 to 49—Average
Below 39—Poor

Assignment 4

The next step in this inventory gives us information about your ability in the essential skills of reading aloud.

Choose a poem or poems (limit your performance to two minutes in length) that you like. Study your material until you are thoroughly familiar with the thought and feeling expressed by the author. Practice reading it aloud many times, until you are sure you are expressing the thought and feeling of the author in a way that may be appreciated by the audience.

When you are called upon, go to the platform and read so that you can be heard; read clearly and distinctly, in a vivid, stimulating manner. Read to the audience, not to yourself; read in a natural style; do not be artificial. There is a certain thrill which comes to both speaker and audience from good literature vividly interpreted.

Begin your performance with brief introductory remarks. You may comment upon the author, the poem, why you like it, and what it means to you. Read your selection from the printed page so that the audience may fully appreciate the "inner, deeper, richer meaning" which the author has to express. You must do more than merely read aloud. You must interpret, simply but effectively, the thought and feeling of the author.

Again this is an important assignment. Do your best. You should work at it for several days ahead of your performance. Give your *Handbook* to your instructor before you read so that he may record his impressions of your reading.

SPEECH INVENTORY NO. 4

Achievement in Reading Aloud

Student _____

Selection _____   Author _____

Comments:

Choice of Material	7	6	5	4	3	2	1
Arrangement of Material	7	6	5	4	3	2	1
Projection of Thought	7	6	5	4	3	2	1
Projection of Emotion	7	6	5	4	3	2	1
Control of Bodily Activity	7	6	5	4	3	2	1
Rhythm	7	6	5	4	3	2	1
Pronunciation	7	6	5	4	3	2	1
Voice Control	7	6	5	4	3	2	1
Audience Response	7	6	5	4	3	2	1

Total score _____

7—Superior
6—Very Good
5—Good
4—Adequate
3—Poor
2—Very Poor
1—Inferior

Distribution

Above 49—Excellent
41 to 49—Good
32 to 40—Average
Below 32—Poor

ASSIGNMENTS

Note: There are some paragraphs of prose from orations or essays, etc., which would serve very well for this assignment. Check with your instructor as to which would be better for you.

Assignment 5

We have already noted your voice as you produced it in the assignment on the basic processes. Most people have adequate phonation, but it won't take long to make another analysis, this time checking items which you might work on.

SPEECH INVENTORY NO. 5

The Process of Phonation (An Individual Diagnosis)

Evaluation								Inadequacies	Faulty	Severe
Quality	7	6	5	4	3	2	1	Quality		
Pitch	7	6	5	4	3	2	1	Muffled		
Duration	7	6	5	4	3	2	1	Metallic		
Intensity	7	6	5	4	3	2	1	Nasal		
Flexibility	7	6	5	4	3	2	1	Denasal		
Comments:								Harsh		
								Hoarse-Husky		
								Breathy		
								Infantile		
								Pitch		
								High		
								Low		
								Inflection pattern		
								Duration		
								Staccato		
								Perseveration		
								Intensity		
								Too weak		
								Too loud		
								Organic abnormality Nature of:		

Student _____

Evaluator _____ Date _____

Write a short exposition on a job that you have had. You may write about a full-time job, a part-time job, or a "job" that you have performed for some group—scouts, fraternity, church, or service club. Write down what you did on this job. Do not write more than 200 words.

Practice reading what you have written. On the day appointed, give your *Handbook* to your instructor as you go to the front of the room to read. Try to read your composition as naturally as possible.

Assignment 6

We have also checked your articulation before, but we have not listened to your speech sounds with planned concentration.

Arranged below are 12 groups of sentences. Each group contains five numbered items which emphasize a certain sound—sounds commonly misarticulated by people who have articulatory problems.

Read the sentences aloud several times before you come to class. Be sure that you can pronounce all the words. When you are called upon, read the designated paragraphs, slowly, clearly, and distinctly. If you are assigned number 1, read item number 1 in each of the groups; if number 2 is assigned to you, read item number 2 in each of the groups, and so on.

Read from the front of the room. Your instructor will check the sounds he hears inaccurately made. All the groups concentrate on a consonant sound. If you make the vowel sounds in an unusual manner, he will note them as you read along through all the sentences.

It may be that your articulation will be affected by an identifiable cause. For example, there may be apparent organic deviations, such as poorly occluded teeth, cleft palate or lip, bothersome tongue, or uncontrolled facial muscles.

Your speech may be marred by faulty rhythm, such as excessive speed of utterance without variety, or too much drawl, extreme hesitation, or excessive repetitions.

Perhaps your problem is having your English speech affected by a foreign language which you speak naturally.

Or perhaps you speak inaccurately as the result of carelessness, slighting of sounds, or oral inactivity.

[s]

1. In accordance with prevailing custom the celebrated congressman closed his office and saw the opening baseball game of the season.

ASSIGNMENTS

2. The professor was surprised at the sustained publicity which he received concerning his theories on business and finance during the banking crisis.

3. The principal of the high school suspended six prominent seniors on a basis of evidence indicating gross misconduct at the senior prom.

4. The secretary, suspicious of the lobbyist, engaged him in conversation, under pretense of an interview, until the senator had left his office through a side entrance.

5. The surgeon was pessimistic concerning the recovery of the sixty-seven year old nurse from a severe illness.

[z]

1. President Theodore Roosevelt shook hands with each of the dignitaries from Brazil congratulating them upon their zest and enthusiasm in so zealously espousing their cause.

2. Thousands of frenzied students zigzagged through the maze of traffic in the busy streets cheering the team which rose to its zenith that day.

3. As the zero hour approached, the soldiers in the war zone were poised for an offensive accompanied by that invisible enemy, poison gas.

4. The zoologist who was chosen to lead the expedition to New Zealand desired to use natives as guides.

5. The Zeppelin flew across the Torrid Zone carrying those citizens of Brazil whose desire was a quick trip home.

[ʌ] and [w]

1. The warden whispered to the deputy that a low whistle was to be the signal for the somewhat ill-timed jail break.

2. When the discussion began, the issue was whether the White House in Washington should be rebuilt in a time when poverty and distress were in existence everywhere.

3. When the attorney asked the witness, "Why did you murder your wife?" he turned white, asked for a glass of water, then waited awhile, before whispering his answer.

4. As winter approached and the wind whistled through the trees, the occupants of the old white house were certain that their hard work during the summer had been worth while.

5. That our well-being is dependent upon the automobile is shown by the fact that, wherever we go, whatever we do, everywhere, the world is literally on wheels.

[θ]

1. As I finished reading the book, I could think of nothing else but the theories of the author regarding youth, wealth, and death.

2. I did not think that the theologist put forth authoritatively or sympatheti-cally the fundamental aspects of the Methodist faith.

ASSIGNMENTS

3. Nothing but the fact that the thermometer stood at thirty degrees below zero prevented Arthur and me from venturing forth to see "Death Takes a Holiday" at the local theatre.

4. Anything that the authority said about growth and health made me thankful that I had heard his theories.

5. Thirty youthful marathon runners threaded their way through the streets of the city from north to south seeking a prize worth one thousand dollars.

[ð]

1. Although the greens were smooth, my brother had trouble with his putting. The ball would roll on either side of the cup rather than into it.

2. "When I breathe rapidly I am bothered with severe chest pains," my brother said. The doctor then bandaged his chest to soothe the affliction.

3. Though the weather was warm and the surface of the lake was smooth, we did breathe easier when we reached the other shore.

4. Our boat drifted hither and thither in the storm. The sight of the water as it seemed to seethe and boil under the lashing of the wind made me writhe in fear.

5. Although I explained to mother that others had fallen likewise, I could not soothe her feelings. Her fall on smooth ice before a large crowd of men had injured her pride.

[ʃ] and [ʒ]

1. The official conclusion of the jury was that the sheriff did not intentionally shoot the garage owner. It was his wish to stop a foolish quarrel.

2. The passengers aboard the British liner rushed to the main deck following the crash. The prestige of the ship's captain and his sharp commands prevented confusion. Upon investigation, conditions were found to be not serious.

3. John Shorey, the County Attorney, assured the judge that he would furnish evidence shortly that would prove that the explosion in the garage that killed Parish was intentional.

4. With the cessation of the barrage, our division advanced shoulder to shoulder under the protection of darkness. The flash of an enemy star shell made it possible for them to distinguish our movement.

5. Thomas Marsh, Treasurer of the City of Shorewind, fought the accusations of his accusers to a finish. A conviction meant loss of prestige for Marsh as well as for those who shielded him.

[tʃ]

1. The hunters, chilled with the cold and very much dismayed, returned empty-handed. As they stretched before the fire that evening, each told of seeing a flock of baby prairie chickens just beyond the orchard, which in each case was left unmolested.

101

2. Much was said concerning the opposition of the French merchants to the importation of Chinese products. They did not wish to purchase goods produced by such cheap labor.

3. The new preacher spoke with unusual charm. His sermons were cherished by young and old, by rich and poor. He achieved success through simplicity of thoughts, words, and speech.

4. Word came to Coach Arthur Chambers that the Larchwood players knew his team's signals. He had one week in which to effect a change. Secret practices were charted. Several watchmen guarded the field.

5. Each debater was asked by his teacher to make a chart on the blackboard which would show comparatively the prices charged for foodstuffs by the chain stores and by the local merchants.

[dʒ]

1. The general raised the question as to just what advantage would be gained if the village of Toul were made a major objective in the next offensive.

2. According to the legend, the gypsies sought revenge against the king because of unjust treatment. They had hoped that he would be generous as a result of their pledge.

3. The stage was set for the trial of the surgeon. The jurors were in their places. A large crowd filled the room. The judge began by objecting to the apparent prejudice of the crowd.

4. A majority of the council approved the budget. The mayor, who had made a pledge to reduce taxes, vetoed it because in his judgment the change in the salary schedule was not justified.

5. The package containing the genuine ransom money was left under the bridge. Just as the agent left the scene a man carrying an object ran into the woods.

[t] and [d]

1. A terrible accident occurred just before dawn at the grade crossing. The Dover limited struck a bus broadside, killed ten persons outright, and severely injured two others.

2. The statement, "United we stand, divided we fall," true at other times in our history, is equally true today. Our present need is leadership that definitely inspires and commands unity.

3. Recent changes in motor car design have tended to increase speed, power, and riding comfort. Floating power, no draft ventilation, knee action, all steel bodies, and the electric hand, are different features advertised.

4. Recently in debate tournaments all over the land, high school students discussed the advisability of direct Federal aid to public education.

5. The complexity of the present political situation tends to increase daily. Opponents of the present order argue that ideals and methods long held sacred are being destroyed.

102

ASSIGNMENTS

[m], [n] and [ŋ]

1. The annual income of the nation has been less than its expenses during the last few years. The problem has been one of finding new methods of raising more money in the face of a sinking volume of business. Our leaders are thankful that business seems to be more normal this year than last.

2. The national banking crisis was met successfully by the President and his advisers. The adoption by Congress of his recommendations for establishing compulsory insurance against loss to depositors came to be one of the prime factors in destroying fear.

3. Several years ago a newspaper correspondent said: "The clank of war machinery rings anew, heralding an impending conflict. Colonial expansion, armament, aggression are the order of the day. Our national policy of neutrality may not protect us from war if it comes."

4. The motion picture industry is still experimenting with new methods of color photography. Judging from the enthusiasm with which most productions filmed in natural color have been received, it ranks as a singular triumph in the development of the cinema.

5. From roving gangs of boys in our large cities come many of our most notorious young outlaws. They commit minor crimes at first but soon gain confidence with each successful attempt. From apprentice gangsters they become hardened criminals, and enemies of the nation.

[l]

1. The new law passed by the city council failed to lower appreciably the cost of electricity to the small consumer as planned.

2. From the top of Indian Lookout Hill one saw in the valley below mile upon mile of freshly cultivated fields broken only by a lazy river winding its way toward the distant bluffs.

3. The nation lost two fine personalities with the death of Will Rogers and Wiley Post in Alaska several years ago. In the last few months the simple plain-spoken philosophy which was so characteristic of Will, and the leadership in aviation which Wiley would have supplied have been sorely missed.

4. The repeal of Prohibition did not solve the liquor problem. It is questioned whether experimental attempts at state and local control, in the hope that the return of the old style saloon generally would be prevented, have been successful.

5. In recent years the relief of distress among the unemployed has increased local, state, and national expenditures greatly. It is said that though unemployment may be lessened its complete elimination is questioned.

[r]

1. With a roar of approval, the Harvard football team rushed onto the field. They were facing a fierce encounter with their old rivals from Princeton.

ASSIGNMENTS

2. The arrival of the troops caused bitter resentment among the crowd of farmers who had gathered to resist the action of the court.

3. The reception arranged for the Byrd expedition on its return from two years of adventure in the Antarctic was a success.

4. Owing to the abnormal rains the streams overflowed their banks and the river rose to flood stage, causing a feeling of general alarm.

5. Reigns of terror in several foreign countries, resulting from racial prejudice, are arousing indignation here and throughout the world.

SPEECH INVENTORY NO. 6

The Process of Articulation (An Individual Diagnosis)

Incorrect Speech Sounds				Other Articulation Problems		
Group	Sound	Severe	Faulty	Problem	Severe	Faulty
1	[s]			Organic		
2	[z]			Teeth		
3	[ʍ] and [w]			Lips		
4	[θ]			Tongue		
5	[ð]			Palates		
6	[ʃ] and [ʒ]			Facial muscles		
7	[tʃ]			Rhythm		
8	[dʒ]			Excessive speed		
9	[t] and [d]			Excessive drawl		
10	[m], [n] and [ŋ]			Jerky		
11	[l]			Foreign accent Nationality:		
12	[r]			Oral inactivity		
Vowels	[ɛ]					
and	[aɪ]					
Diphthongs	[aʊ]					

30   Assignments in speech making

The assignments below are designed to help you develop your skill in the essential skills of speech making. They are cumulative in design, that is, each builds on what was accomplished in the preceding.

Your instructor may wish to vary the procedure from class to class, by eliminating some assignments with some groups, or by repeating assignments with other groups. He may wish to alternate assignments in speech making and reading aloud.

Preparing your speeches. You will, no doubt, be called upon frequently in this course to make speeches. To achieve your best you must prepare each speech carefully. It is wise to extend your preparation over a long rather than a short period of time. Think about the speech, work it over, study it for short periods daily. Follow in order the steps listed below.

1. Choose for your speech a general subject that arises out of a background with which you are familiar.

2. Choose a central thought (a specific phase of this general subject) that can be completely developed in the time allowed. Gather material to support this central thought.

3. Divide this central thought into subordinate points in terms of the material you have gathered.

4. Plan the body of your speech. Arrange the subpoints in an order best suited for the development of your central thought. Choose and arrange the material for the development of your points.

5. Plan your conclusion.

6. Now that you know *what* you must introduce, plan your introduction.

7. Practice the speech aloud many times just as you plan to speak it to the audience.

The rating blanks for these speeches follow *Assignment 16.*

Assignment 7

AIM OF ASSIGNMENT: To learn to identify and use the four parts of a speech.

ASSIGNMENTS

TYPE OF PERFORMANCE: A talk of any type on any subject in which you have a background. *Do not talk about a trip.*

LENGTH OF PERFORMANCE: Not more than two minutes.

REFERENCE MATERIAL: Study *Organization of Material*, Section 12, Part II of this *Speech Handbook*.

SPECIFIC METHOD: Prepare the speech according to the seven steps listed in the introduction to this section.

SUGGESTIONS: Choose interesting material. Avoid worrying about the mechanics of delivery. *Make the four parts stand out clearly.*

Assignment 8

AIM OF ASSIGNMENT: To learn to formulate the central thought of a speech and use it correctly.

TYPE OF PERFORMANCE: A talk of any type on any subject with which you are familiar. *Do not talk about a trip,* because there is seldom a central thought when you tell what you did from day to day on a trip.

LENGTH OF PERFORMANCE: To be determined by the class.

REFERENCE MATERIAL: Review *Choice of Thought*, Section 10, and *Organization of Material,* Section 12 of this *Handbook.*

SPECIFIC METHOD: Prepare according to the seven steps in the introduction to this section. Write out the central thought several times, until it is phrased to suit you and according to the principles.

REPEATED FUNCTIONS: Be sure that the speech has four parts as in *Assignment* 7.

SUGGESTIONS: Choose interesting material. Avoid worrying about the mechanics of delivery, and make the four parts stand out clearly. Be sure that the central thought is stated at least three times.

Assignment 9

AIM OF ASSIGNMENT: To learn to divide the central thought into subpoints around which the material and details may be arranged, and to state these subpoints properly.

TYPE OF PERFORMANCE: A talk of any type on any subject with which you are familiar. *Do not talk about a trip.*

LENGTH OF PERFORMANCE: Two to four minutes.

REFERENCE MATERIAL: Review *Choice of Thought*, Section 10.

ASSIGNMENTS

SPECIFIC METHOD: Prepare the speech according to the seven steps mentioned before. Divide your central thought into two or three points, no more. Name point one, *First*, and point two, *Second*, and so on. Refer to the points while making your speech as *First, Second,* and so forth.

REPEATED FUNCTIONS: Be sure that your speech has four distinct parts, that the central thought conforms to the principles and that it is stated at least three times.

SUGGESTIONS: Choose a subject that lends itself to division into two or three points. Choose interesting material. Don't worry about the mechanics of delivery. Make the four parts and especially the central thought and subpoints stand out clearly.

Assignment 10

AIM OF ASSIGNMENT: To learn to relate and connect your material, your subpoints, your central thought, by use of the techniques of repetition, transition, and summary; also, to learn to use the blackboard.

TYPE OF PERFORMANCE: Draw a diagram on the blackboard designed to give the audience a specific bit of information.

LENGTH OF PERFORMANCE: Not more than five minutes.

REFERENCE MATERIAL: Review items relative to the *body* of the speech under *Organization of Material*, Section 12.

SPECIFIC METHOD: Let the information you wish to give be the central thought of your speech. State it as such. Divide it into only two points, if possible. After you have developed your first point state, repeat, summarize in one sentence what you have thus far accomplished. Example (from a speech about a football play): "In brief, deception in the *option play* is brought about by _____" (here the speaker quickly traces over the diagram the movements of players *a, b, c, d,* etc.,). Your next sentence should repeat in a phrase your first point then lead into and connect it to the second point. *Example:* "Now that it is clear that deception is an important aspect of the *option play* let us consider the importance of speed in its execution." Your next sentence should repeat the general reference to speed, specifically. *Example:* "Speed is the second important factor in the success of the *option play*." Repeat the above procedure after the second point has been completed and lead into the conclusion. *Example:* "The element of speed contributes to the success of the *option play* then, as follows: (here the speaker briefly illustrates on the diagram what he has said about "speed"). This factor of speed when combined with deception makes the *option play* useful in the attack of any football team. And so, when you see a team begin a play in this manner (refer to diagram), with the movement of the players in this manner (refer to diagram), with the quarterback— (etc., etc.), and the ball is carried down the field for 20 yards you will know that deception and speed have collaborated successfully in making the *option play* an important weapon in the offensive team's attack."

REPEATED FUNCTIONS: Your speech should have four parts, a central thought correctly stated and repeated and two subpoints correctly stated.

SUGGESTIONS: Choose an interesting subject that lends itself to picturization and that has two obvious points for which the diagram may be conveniently utilized. Do not explain something about which everybody knows.

Make the diagram large enough to be seen by all. While you are drawing it keep talking about it to the audience. Make this discussion part of the introduction. Look at the audience occasionally. Don't talk *to* the blackboard. Do not stand in front of the diagram when you explain it. Stand at the side, to the right of the diagram if you are right-handed. Actually use the diagram to make your points clear. Do not be afraid of repeating your explanation too often.

Assignment 11

AIM OF ASSIGNMENT: To learn to conclude your speech properly, to use the conclusion as an aid in emphasizing, in making your points clear, and in adapting them to the audience; further, to use the blackboard again.

TYPE OF PERFORMANCE: Use the same type of speech as in *Assignment 10*. Use two sections of the blackboard this time. Diagram point 1 on one board and point 2 on the second. You might even separate the two sections on which you draw by a blank section between. In this way you will have to move about as you talk.

ASSIGNMENTS

LENGTH OF PERFORMANCE: Not more than five minutes.

REFERENCE MATERIAL: Review items relative to the *conclusion* under *Organization of Material*.

SPECIFIC METHOD: Divide the central thought into the two points you wish to illustrate by the diagram. If you have more than two subpoints, you will need more sections of blackboard on which to draw your diagrams. After you have worked out the body of the speech, plan the conclusion to lift out and emphasize the two points which you have made. Relate these points to the central thought, showing how you have used them as definite steps in its development. Adapt and apply the point of the central thought to the audience, making it a part of their knowledge. Relate it to the activities of their every day life. You must do more than repeat and summarize.

REPEATED FUNCTION: Your speech should have four parts, a correctly stated and repeated central thought, and two subpoints correctly stated. You should use repetitions, transitions, summaries as outlined in *Assignment 10*.

SUGGESTIONS: Be sure that your subject is new and interesting. Watch your audience carefully, during the body of the speech, and determine from their reactions if your explanation is clear. If they seem to express uncertainty do not hesitate to repeat those parts of the explanation which seem difficult. Be as brief, yet complete, as possible.

Assignment 12

AIM OF ASSIGNMENT: To learn to introduce your speech properly, to make your introductory remarks serve the functions of providing a background for, arousing interest in, and leading up to the central thought of your speech.

TYPE OF PERFORMANCE: Select and bring to class an object, a picture, a map, a work of art, a toy, an instrument, a tool, an appliance, a product, which you can display to the audience. Be sure it is large enough to be seen. If it can be taken apart, put together again, so much the better. Do not use a familiar object such as a pencil, or a fountain pen unless you can make an unusually interesting speech about it.

LENGTH OF PERFORMANCE: Not more than four minutes.

ASSIGNMENTS

REFERENCE MATERIAL: Review items relative to the *introduction* under *Organization of Material*.

SPECIFIC METHOD: Let the information you wish to give about the object be the central thought of your speech. State it definitely. Divide it into two or three points. If you have followed the seven recommended steps in preparing your speech, the central thought, the body, and the conclusion are now planned. Obviously you need to introduce the object to the audience as well as your speech about it. Decide what historical or background material you need to give concerning it, what personal remarks you need to make about it, what you need to do to interest your audience in it, what new terms you need to define in order to discuss it.

Arrange your material in such an order that the audience is led directly and naturally into a consideration of the central thought. Plan each step carefully, rehearse it until you can present it smoothly.

REPEATED FUNCTIONS: Your speech should have four parts, a carefully and correctly stated central thought, two or three well-stated points connected by transitions, emphasized by repetitions and summaries, and a conclusion which reiterates and adapts the subpoints to the central thought, the central thought to the audience.

SUGGESTIONS: Avoid simply holding the object, display it, hold it up, walk down to the audience, walk among them displaying it so that all may see. Manipulate it, take it apart, put it together several times, actually use it as a device for making your points clear. Do not let the audience pass the object from person to person. It distracts from your talk.

Avoid a long, trite, ordinary, pointless introduction. Begin with the familiar and work to the unfamiliar. Make your introduction serve a definite purpose, get you off to a good start, make the audience desire to hear what is to follow.

Assignment 13

AIM OF ASSIGNMENT: To experiment with the development of effectiveness in projection to the audience through telling a well-known story in your own words.

TYPE OF PERFORMANCE: Select a child's story which you remember and which you used to like as a child, such as *Red Riding Hood, The*

Three Bears, The Three Little Pigs, or *Peter Rabbit.* Be sure that there are at least two characters in the story who speak one to another. Condense the story and tell it to the audience in your own words. Endeavor to amuse them with the characters, the events, the fun which is in the story.

LENGTH OF PERFORMANCE: Not more than three minutes.

SPECIFIC METHOD: Select your story, then condense it. Plan to present only the most important details, the most important characters, the most amusing speeches of the characters. Experiment with the voices of the different characters. Exaggerate them to get the exaggerated ideas of the story. Remember that these stories are sheer exaggeration and must be so treated. Make the emotional aspects of the story vivid, thrilling, startling. Arrange the points of the story and the details of its development in climactic order.

REPEATED FUNCTIONS: Make each word and phrase vivid. Let the audience feel your endeavor to make the story live through interpreting the "inner, deeper, richer meanings" of it. Make brief introductory remarks to the audience before you begin the story.

SUGGESTIONS: Approach your performance and your audience with a spirit of good fun. Look at them, talk to them, laugh with them, whether it be at you or the story. Watch your audience; be sure you are stimulating them the way you intend. From time to time during your preparation, read aloud *Sojo* in Section 37 of the Appendix, to experiment with voice control.

Assignment 14

AIM OF ASSIGNMENT: To experiment with the development of effectiveness in projection to the audience through relating a thrilling experience of your own.

TYPE OF PERFORMANCE: Select the most vivid, thrilling experience you have had, one that affected you intensely and emotionally. Relate the experience and reproduce for your audience your feelings just as you felt them.

LENGTH OF PERFORMANCE: Not over three minutes.

REFERENCE MATERIAL: Study *Use of Language,* Section 13.

SPECIFIC METHOD: Go over in your mind the experience as you remember it. Select those details essential to the development for the

111

audience of the thrill you had. Arrange them in order of climax. Carefully plan each sentence in series from beginning to end. Choose only the most vivid and specific words. Let the emotions you felt at the time dominate your behavior as you speak. Experiment with your presentation of it until you are able to make it real, vivid, and startling. The audience must follow every phase of it with anxiety and there should be a feeling of relief on their part, when you have finished, such as you felt in the original experience. Introduce the story with brief remarks; likewise, conclude with a few brief remarks appropriate to the situation.

REPEATED FUNCTIONS: Exaggerate sufficiently your interpretation of the experience so that the audience is aware of the depth of your feelings. Estimate the type of reaction your audience should give to the story. Plan to secure it. Try as hard as you can to define the meaning of each word and phrase for the audience through use of your voice. Look at them, talk to them, be thrilled with them. Watch their reactions; if they do not behave as you think they should, project more intently.

SUGGESTIONS: If you have had no thrilling experience which you wish to tell, use an imaginary one or tell one of which you have heard or read. This is more difficult to do well since you have not experienced it yourself and consequently may not be able to feel it emotionally. Strive hard for that audience response characterized by "a room so quiet you could hear a pin drop," a sigh of relief at the end, with applause.

Assignment 15

AIM OF ASSIGNMENT: To repeat what was attempted in *Assignment 14* by use of a humorous experience.

TYPE OF PERFORMANCE: Select the most embarrassing or the most humorous experience you have ever had. Tell the experience and reproduce for your audience your feelings at the time, exactly as you felt them.

LENGTH OF PERFORMANCE: Not more than three minutes.

SPECIFIC METHOD: Refer to *Assignment 14* and in your preparation follow the points mentioned therein.

ASSIGNMENTS

REPEATED FUNCTIONS: Exaggerate your interpretation of the experience to produce a humorous effect. Make each word and phrase, as vocally expressed, define your thought and feeling. Follow your audience reaction; adapt your style to it.

SUGGESTIONS: If you have no humorous or embarrassing experience to tell about, make up one or tell one of which you have read or heard. If you do the latter you must get into the spirit of it and present it as if you had experienced it. Use every available method to build up your experience and get your audience to laugh at its humorous elements.

Assignment 16

AIM OF ASSIGNMENT: To experiment with the projection of an opinion of your own to the audience.

TYPE OF PERFORMANCE: Select for a speech a subject upon which you have a deep conviction, belief, or opinion, the type of subject which makes you angry or "see red" when it is mentioned. Present your opinion with all the depth of feeling which you have upon the subject. Make this feeling apparent to the audience. Transfer it to them.

LENGTH OF PERFORMANCE: Not more than three minutes.

REFERENCE MATERIAL: Review *Choice of Thought* and *Organization of Material* in this *Handbook*.

SPECIFIC METHOD: State the opinion you wish to present in the form of the central thought of your speech. Prepare your speech as suggested in previous assignments, following the seven-step pattern. Practice its presentation in order that you may project your feelings clearly and effectively. Be more interested in making your audience aware of your opinion and your feelings toward it than of the reasons for your belief.

REPEATED FUNCTIONS: The speech should meet the test of a well-organized speech as outlined previously. Be sure that the central thought is well stated. Exaggerate the interpretation of your feelings. Follow your audience reaction. Control your projection in terms of their reaction.

SUGGESTIONS: Use the first person when you speak. Fill your speech with personal phrases such as, "I think," or "I believe." Concentrate on your central thought. Be sure that you make your point of view clear and emphatic. Avoid generalization that is not directly related to your central thought.

ACHIEVEMENT IN SPEECH MAKING

Assignment No. _____   Student _____

Date _____   Subject _____

Comments:

Choice of Subject	7	6	5	4	3	2	1
Choice of Thought	7	6	5	4	3	2	1
Choice of Material	7	6	5	4	3	2	1
Organization of Material	7	6	5	4	3	2	1
Use of Language	7	6	5	4	3	2	1
Projection to the Audience	7	6	5	4	3	2	1
Control of Bodily Activity	7	6	5	4	3	2	1
Rhythm	7	6	5	4	3	2	1
Pronunciation	7	6	5	4	3	2	1
Voice Control	7	6	5	4	3	2	1
Audience Response	7	6	5	4	3	2	1

Total score _____

7—Superior
6—Very Good   Distribution
5—Good
4—Adequate   Above 60—Excellent
3—Poor   50 to 60—Good
2—Very Poor   39 to 49—Average
1—Inferior   Below 39—Poor

Evaluator _____

31   Assignments in reading aloud

The assignments below are designed to help you develop your skill in the essentials of reading aloud.

Again, as with the assignments on speech making, your instructor may wish to vary the procedure with your class by making a pertinent selection of the exercises suitable to your needs and abilities. Or he may wish to repeat any of significant value.

To be assured of a measure of success, check your selection of poems to read with your instructor. He will help you know whether your poem will help meet the aim of the assignment.

ASSIGNMENTS

Assignment 17

AIM OF ASSIGNMENT: To aid you in projection of thought in reading aloud.

TYPE OF PERFORMANCE: Select a poem or poems you like, that your audience will like to hear you read aloud. Select a poem that has significant thought content. Avoid narrative poetry, the type that tells a story. It would be best to have a serious poem. *Read from the printed page.*

LENGTH OF PERFORMANCE: Not more than two minutes.

REFERENCE MATERIAL: Read *Projection of Thought*, Section 22.

SPECIFIC METHOD: Study your poem intently. Know the meaning of each phrase and word. Be able to express the central thought in your own words. Be sure you can read it in phrases, regardless of line scheme or rhyme scheme. It would be good for your reading if you were to type out your manuscript. If you do, it is not necessary to adhere to the line arrangement of the original. You are aiming to project thought. Decide on places where you should pause. Mark those places. Select key words to receive emphasis. Underline these words. Practice reading *That Pup* in Section 38, trying to achieve a spontaneity in your reading.

SUGGESTIONS: Prepare an introduction in which you mention the title, the author, and the central thought of the poem. Practice reading from manuscript.

The rating blanks to be used for these assignments in the basic skills of reading aloud follow Assignment 20.

Assignment 18

AIM OF ASSIGNMENT: To approach the problem of *projection of emotion.*

TYPE OF PERFORMANCE: Select a poem you like, one that your audience will like to hear you read aloud. Choose a simple narrative type of poem with thought and emotion expressed in broad sweeps through the use of many vivid and colorful words. It may be either serious or humorous. *Read from the printed page.*

ASSIGNMENTS

LENGTH OF PERFORMANCE: Not more than two minutes.

REFERENCE MATERIAL: Study Projection of Emotion, Section 23.

SPECIFIC METHOD: Study the poem to ascertain its "inner, deeper, richer meanings." Estimate the reaction that the listener should give to the poem, its words, phrases, and stanzas. Plan your interpretation to secure that reaction. Try as hard as you can to define each word through the use of your voice by varying pitch, intensity, quality, and duration to suit your purpose. Make each word ring with its fullest meaning.

REPEATED FUNCTIONS: Make sure of the meaning of all words and phrases. Mark your manuscript for pauses and emphasis.

SUGGESTIONS: Study the reactions of your audience. Estimate their interest and how closely they follow you. If they are restless or bored, you are not projecting adequately. You must sense a feeling of interest on their part. They must respond to you and the ideas of the poem with real interest and enthusiasm. Avoid merely reading aloud, in which you simply pronounce the words. Read *to* and *for* the audience.

Assignment 19

AIM OF ASSIGNMENT: To experiment further with the development of effectiveness in *projection of thought* and *emotion*.

TYPE OF PERFORMANCE: Choose a different type of poem for this performance. If you used a serious poem before, use a humorous poem this time. *Read from the printed page.*

LENGTH OF PERFORMANCE: Not more than two minutes.

REFERENCE MATERIAL: Review *Projection of Thought* and *Projection of Emotion*, Sections 22 and 23.

SPECIFIC METHOD: Repeat the method used in *Assignments 17* and *18*. Introduce your poem with a few brief remarks stating the name of the poem, its author, its source, and your reason for reading it. Try to stimulate your audience so that they respond with a great deal of interest and enthusiasm.

REPEATED FUNCTIONS: Make each word and phrase vivid with thought and feeling. Make the audience aware of your endeavor to interpret the meaning attached to each word.

116

ASSIGNMENTS

SUGGESTIONS: Practice the poem aloud many times. Become so familiar with it that you need only refer to the book for the exact wording of the poem. Experiment with different effects as you practice. In the production of your effects try the use of different pitch, quality, intensity, and duration changes. *Experiment as you practice.* Experiment with your audience as you read. Watch your audience for their response. If they do not respond, project more intently.

Assignment 20

AIM OF ASSIGNMENT: To give further experience in the development of a style of projection to the audience, by combining speaking and reading in one performance.

TYPE OF PERFORMANCE: Select a poem, several quotations from a long poem, or poems that express a thought you wish to present to the audience. Prepare a speech with this thought as the central thought and use the poetry as your material in developing the thought. Thus, you read and speak in the same performance.

LENGTH OF PERFORMANCE: Not more than three minutes.

REFERENCE MATERIAL: Review *Organization of Material* and *Projection of Thought* as outlined in this *Handbook.*

SPECIFIC METHOD: Follow in preparation of this speech the method you have previously learned. Practice reading the poetry aloud until you are confident of your ability to project its "inner, deeper, richer meanings." Practice the entire performance until you make your speaking as vivid and colorful as your reading. Interpret every word and phrase with its proper emotional value. Let your own feelings be expressed completely whether you use your own words or the words of another.

REPEATED FUNCTIONS: Your speech should have four parts, and be built together as a unit. You should consider the reaction you wish to gain from your audience and strive to accomplish it. Exaggerate your interpretation sufficiently to make it clear.

SUGGESTIONS: Make use of proper transitions, in which you relate to your main thought the points involved in the poetry you read. Actually use the poetry in developing your thought. Try and project as well when you speak as when you read. Don't let a noticeable difference be apparent.

ASSIGNMENTS

ACHIEVEMENT IN READING ALOUD

Assignment No. _____   Student _____

Date _____   Selection _____   Author _____

Comments:

Choice of Material	7	6	5	4	3	2	1
Arrangement of Material	7	6	5	4	3	2	1
Projection of Thought	7	6	5	4	3	2	1
Projection of Emotion	7	6	5	4	3	2	1
Control of Bodily Activity	7	6	5	4	3	2	1
Rhythm	7	6	5	4	3	2	1
Pronunciation	7	6	5	4	3	2	1
Voice Control	7	6	5	4	3	2	1
Audience Response	7	6	5	4	3	2	1

Total score _____

7—Superior
6—Very Good
5—Good
4—Adequate
3—Poor
2—Very Poor
1—Inferior

Distribution

Above 49—Excellent
41 to 49—Good
32 to 40—Average
Below 32—Poor

Evaluator _____

PART SIX

Projects in Speaking
and Reading

32   The long speech

Among the objectives for a beginning course in speech are improving
the basic processes of speech, and increasing the student's ability in
the basic skills of speech making and reading aloud. To do this we
usually make assignments calling for very short performances. This
makes for *speaking readiness*. It enables the student to meet speaking
situations with enough understanding and "know how" to have a
go at his task with some degree of confidence.

In addition to the short assignments we make, we often wish that
some of our students, who are ready for more advanced work, might
have an opportunity to go on in developing the art of speaking. Therefore, we present now a series of assignments that will give these advanced students, who have already acquired some assurance and
poise in their speaking, an opportunity to do longer, more careful,
and more intense planning, preparation, and rehearsal than before.

In addition, the advanced student will consider his audience more
closely. He need not be as much concerned about his own participation as a beginner. He can concentrate on eliciting desired responses
from his listeners.

We do not intend through these assignments to give specific training in making speeches to meet particular occasions, such as the speech of welcome, the speech of presentation, the speech of acceptance, the after-dinner speech, reading the minutes of meetings of the club, or reading the scripture lesson for your young people's religious group. Neither do we plan to train anyone to do an oration for intercollegiate participation.

We do plan to encourage through the basic assignments a readiness to speak. And through these advanced assignments we hope you will learn that you too can give a good talk if you are willing to make the effort.

Assignment 21

The speech to inform.

AIM OF ASSIGNMENT: To provide the listener with information on a specific subject through presenting in detail, rehearsing industriously, and speaking extemporaneously an informative talk in a natural, spontaneous form. The listeners must be able to comprehend easily, be very much interested, and be able to remember what you said.

LENGTH OF PERFORMANCE: Between seven and ten minutes.

METHOD AND SUGGESTIONS: Consider carefully the skills of speech making, as follows:

Choice of subject: Remember that your audience will be your classmates and the occasion will be your class meeting, unless you and your instructor make arrangements for presenting the speech at a different time and place. Some groups like to meet in the evening, in some place other than the classroom, in groups of about eight students, devoting about an hour and a half to the meeting.

The topic you choose may require that you do any or all of the following: explain a process, a thing, or an idea; develop a principle or a theory; paint a word picture using words of vivid imagery; relate the events or series of events of a significant happening; or report the results of a survey or investigation. The speech should contain information that you are reasonably sure your audience does not already have. You should know a lot about it to begin with, know where you can find more, and be very much interested in it yourself.

Choice of thought.   You need a central thought for this speech, as for any other. It should be clear and brief. It should be divided into points—probably not less than three nor more than five.

Choice of material.   Decide on the type of supporting material you will use. If you decide to use statistics, get them. If you plan to use statements from authority, find them. Select your materials with your audience in mind. Make a sincere effort to use some of your information in the form of visual aids. This means charts, diagrams, mounted drawings and pictures. Be sure they are large enough to be seen from the back of the room.

Organization of material.   Think out carefully the order of arrangement you plan to use—time, space, topical, or otherwise. Think out your transitional devices very carefully. Decide on the type of conclusion you wish to have, and plan it. Do the same for the introduction. Write out the first 35 words you will say after you have been introduced by the chairman. Do the same for the last words you will utter before you sit down.

Use of language.   This speech is to be extemporaneous, to be sure. Yet there are places in any speech where you want to say exactly what you mean, in the best language you can plan. Such places are at the opening, as you state the central thought and the subpoints, as you make your transitions, and as you finish. Be sure you know whether you must use any unusual or technical terms. If you must, be sure to include clear explanations of each, or simplifications for them.

Projection to the audience.   Plan for this speech. Consider where you will stand, the position you feel would be best for you. Then practice these things. Ask someone who is interested in the progress you are making to hear you practice your talk. Practice by yourself several times, and then speak before this person who will give you his appraisal of the talk. Your instructor would be your best critic, but a classmate could help, or a member of your family. If it is a member of your family, you will want to "brief" him on what you are trying to do.

Be sure to "speak up" in the practice session, and look at your listener. Use as much voice as you think you will need when you are speaking to the audience for whom you have planned this talk. You cannot do this until you are ready, so be sure to practice several times first by yourself.

Control of bodily activity. Your activity in moving about and gesturing should arise out of your thought and feeling as you speak. By having visual aids you will enhance your control of bodily activity. Have the aids hung or placed before you begin to speak. Do not mention them until you are ready to use them. Uncover them as you need them. Re-cover them or remove them when you are through with them—usually during the speech, as you finish with them. Practice pointing out the features of the visual aids. Use the hand nearest the device as you stand to one side or the other.

Rhythm. It is often a good idea to intentionally increase the rate of your speaking in order to present an enthusiastic appearance to the audience and insure their attention. At the same time do not forget that the pause, and variety in emphasis and inflections are among your finest attributes to interestingness.

Pronunciation. Have your audience in mind. Do not allow yourself to use words you are unsure of. Many of your classmates will not respond favorably if you mispronounce words.

Voice control. Here again, think of your audience. They like to hear without effort. Be sure to speak a little louder than you sometimes do—unless you have been told that your voice is naturally too loud. In that rare event, make a sincere effort to cut down on volume. As you practice, try repeating some phrases several times in order to make sure that you are presenting the meaning you want to present in the best manner you are capable.

Audience response. This is important. Think about it. When you practice, keep your audience in mind. Talk with your instructor about the response they are likely to make. Think about how they might respond, and plan for what you will do. If you see them craning their necks to see your visual aids, hold them up for better viewing. Or sometimes it is good to ask if they can see or hear.

Note: The evaluation sheets for the talks in this section follow *Assignment 22.*

Assignment 22

A speech to persuade

AIM OF ASSIGNMENT: To provide practice under close supervision in the gathering, evaluation, and use of evidence (examples, statistics, testimony) to convince others of the soundness of a point of view which you hold.

LENGTH OF PERFORMANCE: From seven to ten minutes.

METHOD AND SUGGESTIONS: Probably you use persuasion throughout life more than you use exposition (giving information). Think of what you do during the day: you try to get your car pool to be on time in the morning, you try to get a friend to go over to the student center with you to get a cup of coffee before the next class, you try to get a student to lend you his notes for the class you missed, you try to get your father to lend you his car for the evening. All of these efforts to influence the action of others are a form of persuasion. Think of the times you argue a point, trying to get someone to agree with you. This is persuasion.

This assignment calls for your best efforts, again following the guiding considerations of the essential skills of speech making.

Choice of subject. Select your subject carefully. Before making your final selection, talk with your instructor to make sure you are on the right track. Pick a topic from among the many problems of international, national, state, local, or campus scope. Be sure there is controversy about it, and that you have heard some arguments on both sides. When you are sure that you have a problem that has two sides, think about it with a sincere effort to decide which side you really believe in. Then make sure that information on your side is available. For this speech you will not be able to call entirely on your own experiences and information.

Choice of thought. You know which side of the argument you are on. Now state what you believe in definite, clear terms. This statement becomes your central thought. Make it specific. Let it clearly ask your audience to believe something. For example, do not state your central thought like this: "The voting age should be changed." Make it specific, like this: "The voting age for all American citizens should be lowered to 18 years."

Then set down all the "reasons" you can think of. These "reasons" become the main points of your speech. If you have more than five you probably will not have time to prove each one. It would be better to combine some, or leave some out, and do a good job of proving the important ones you have settled on.

Choice of material. You will need to collect evidence for each of your reasons. You will need to read on the subject, searching for facts, statistics, examples, illustrations, and quotations, for each reason. You want your audience to agree with you. They won't, if all you can do is make assertions without backing them up with evidence. But if you have the facts and figures, they will be more likely to accept your proof.

Organization of material. You will need to arrange your main points in the best possible order. The same is true for the supporting material and the details of the supporting material.

When you have assembled all the evidence for one "reason" and have arranged it, plan a summary of it, showing what you have accomplished. This is a type of transition to the next main "reason."

Plan your conclusion carefully, making sure that it repeats all your main "reasons," which led you to the point of view that you have, and that you expressed in your central thought. Finally, re-state your point.

Plan your introduction to show the importance of the problem that you are going to discuss. Tell something of the background of the problem—how it started, how you are interested in it, how the audience is affected by it—and then state your central idea and point out the main reasons for your position.

Get your argument down on paper in the form of an outline—called a "brief" in argumentation. Show your "brief" to your instructor for approval before you begin rehearsing your speech.

Use of language. In this speech you must use exact, forceful, clear words. Omit vague words unless you define them for your listeners. Be sure that you have the central thought and main points carefully worded so that they say exactly what you want them to say. When you rehearse, insist that you present these points in the words you planned. Your audience is not likely to agree unless you use unmistakable language.

Projection to the audience. Sincerity is the key to your success here. If you are sincere you will be able to practice a well-prepared, well-documented speech. If you are sincere you will be able to rehearse a speech that expresses your own convictions. Keep this sincerity.

Be enthusiastic without bombast. Step up the rate of some of the delivery without ranting. Be loud without shouting.

Again, as in the speech to inform, ask someone to listen to a rehearsal. Talk *to* this critic, not *at* him. It is hard, but it will be easier to talk to your audience later, when you speak to them.

Control of bodily activity. Moving about the platform and gesturing are part of speaking. During your early rehearsals exaggerate your movement and gestures. Then as you go on rehearsing, be selective, just as you are selective in your use of words. Just because you are enthusiastic, do not let it run away with you to where you fling your arms wildly. Be sincerely enthusiastic.

Rhythm. Again you may speak a little faster than usual. Lots of persuaders do, especially when they are as well prepared as you want to be for this speech. But keep your speaking rhythm controlled. Be careful of just racing along. Remember the pause, and variety.

Pronunciation. Make sure of the pronunciation of the words you use.

Voice control. Sometimes speakers tend to raise their pitch when they are earnestly arguing. Be careful that your voice does not reach a high pitch and stay there. Practice making your voice do what you want it to do. In the enthusiasm of your argument, do not forget that an effective voice will help dispose an audience favorably to you and to your argument.

Audience response. Can you anticipate the reaction of your audience? You want them to agree with you. But that is often very difficult. Be content to think that you may influence a few members of the class to agree with you, or at least to be less opposed to your point of view.

Talk with your instructor about the possible attitude of your audience. Keep it in mind as you rehearse and as you deliver the speech.

ACHIEVEMENT IN SPEECH MAKING

Assignment No. _____   Student _____

Date _____   Subject _____

Comments:

Choice of Subject	7	6	5	4	3	2	1
Choice of Thought	7	6	5	4	3	2	1
Choice of Material	7	6	5	4	3	2	1
Organization of Material	7	6	5	4	3	2	1
Use of Language	7	6	5	4	3	2	1
Projection to the Audience	7	6	5	4	3	2	1
Control of Bodily Activity	7	6	5	4	3	2	1
Rhythm	7	6	5	4	3	2	1
Pronunciation	7	6	5	4	3	2	1
Voice Control	7	6	5	4	3	2	1
Audience Response	7	6	5	4	3	2	1

Total score _____

7—Superior
6—Very Good
5—Good
4—Adequate
3—Poor
2—Very Poor
1—Inferior

Distribution

Above 60—Excellent
50 to 60—Good
39 to 49—Average
Below 39—Poor

Evaluator _____

ACHIEVEMENT IN SPEECH MAKING

Assignment No. _____   Student _____

Date _____   Subject _____

Comments:

Choice of Subject	7	6	5	4	3	2	1
Choice of Thought	7	6	5	4	3	2	1
Choice of Material	7	6	5	4	3	2	1
Organization of Material	7	6	5	4	3	2	1
Use of Language	7	6	5	4	3	2	1
Projection to the Audience	7	6	5	4	3	2	1
Control of Bodily Activity	7	6	5	4	3	2	1
Rhythm	7	6	5	4	3	2	1
Pronunciation	7	6	5	4	3	2	1
Voice Control	7	6	5	4	3	2	1
Audience Response	7	6	5	4	3	2	1

Total score _____

7—Superior
6—Very Good
5—Good   Distribution
4—Adequate
3—Poor   Above 60—Excellent
2—Very Poor   50 to 60—Good
1—Inferior   39 to 49—Average
                                Below 39—Poor

Evaluator _____

33   The longer oral reading

It is likely that most of your opportunities to read aloud will call for short readings. Such, for example, as reading the minutes of a meeting, or reading the Scriptures.

There may be an occasion, however, when you will be called upon to present a special feature at your club meeting. In that event the following assignments of the longer reading may help you face those occasions with greater confidence and poise. Besides, it just may be that you might find a rather keen interest in reading aloud, and want to take more course work in interpretation.

Assignment 23

Reading prose aloud

AIM OF THE ASSIGNMENT: To perfect your skill in projection of thought through intense rehearsal in reading aloud a prose selection from the printed page with special attention to phrasing, rhythm, and emphasis.

LENGTH OF PERFORMANCE: Seven to ten minutes.

METHOD AND SUGGESTIONS: We recommend this type of activity for nearly anyone. Children love to be read to—perhaps as much as they enjoy watching television. Others in the family enjoy listening to people read well. The entertainment world has seen successful examples of reading from the public platform during recent years. And some of our outstanding readers, like Charles Laughton, read as part of television programs.

As you prepare this reading, keep the basic skills of reading aloud in mind:

Choice of material. From a current, adult magazine, select an article which is primarily expository or descriptive, not narrative, and which, if read well, will be of interest to the audience. Unless otherwise planned, your audience will likely be your classmates, and the place your classroom. You may enjoy it more if you meet in the evening and use a small auditorium.

The article should be between 1000 and 1500 words. That is about 100 lines of print on a book-size page. Or, it is about 4 or 5 pages of printing.

Perhaps your selection is longer. Then cut it down to a 10-minute length.

Arrangement of material: After you have not more than 10 minutes of material ready to read, plan your introductory remarks. Keep your audience in mind as you prepare these remarks. If you have cut out portions of the article in order to get it within the time limits, you may wish to plan some comments to connect the portions that you have chosen to read.

Projection of thought. Since this is not a dramatic reading, your greatest concern is to get meaning across to your audience. Phrasing and emphasis are most important in this process.

Study the material silently, to make positively sure that you know the meaning of all words. Now, find out if you can read it aloud, getting the meaning yourself. Read it to yourself—aloud. Is it easy to group words together as you read, or do you read word after word? If you do the latter, you must keep rehearsing it over and over until you read groups of words. Meaning is projected through groups of words, not word by word. Note passages that you do not seem to understand clearly as you hear yourself reading aloud. Do something about those passages. Continue to read them until you hear yourself reading groups of words meaningfully. Or leave out that passage, putting an explanatory comment in its place.

Now ask someone to listen to you practice aloud. Ask him to note any words that seem to need more emphasis in order to get meaning across. Try this: look at the last paragraph of the article. Read the first sentence aloud. Did your reading seem to bring out the complete meaning of that paragraph as you understand it? Now read the first sentence (or any other that you identify as the topic sentence) of the next to last paragraph. Then read the second from the last paragraph topic sentence. Continue reading one sentence from each paragraph from the end of the article to the beginning. This will force you to read the single sentence trying to get the complete meaning of the entire paragraph into your reading. As you continue to practice the selection from beginning to end, try to give emphasis to those sentences you have been studying especially, just as you did in the study exercises.

Projection of emotion. The main thing here is sincerity and earnestness. Have the desire to communicate the idea of the author to the listeners. If there is emotional content, your sincerity and desire will probably help it come through.

Rhythm. Again we recommend a good lively rate for your selection. Do not race with it. But do not be ponderously slow, either.

Use pauses. Read an idea briskly, then pause. Then go on, perhaps at a different rate. Remember that you need not always pause

129

where periods or commas are printed. And sometimes you may wish to pause where no punctuation is printed.

Pronunciation. You must pronounce every word correctly. You are reading the words of another and he is entitled to have his words given correct pronunciation. In your own speeches you might take the liberty of being "folksy," as some very popular television entertainers have done, but when you are reading the words of an author, you do not have that privilege.

Voice control. It is through inflections in pitch and other marks of variety in duration, quality, and intensity, that you will bring out the "inner, deeper, richer meanings" of the selection you are presenting to your audience. You must rehearse to do this. Try recording some of your selection on a tape recorder. Hear it played back. Does it show that you are using a vigorous, energetic presentation? Does it present you as speaking sincerely and earnestly, making the thought of the author predominant? Practice several times with the recorder.

Audience response. Watch your audience as you read. Of course, you will be so familiar with your material that you will not have to look at your manuscript more than occasionally. Are they alert and continuously attentive? Do they give evidence that they understand what you are reading?

Note: The *Achievement in Reading Aloud* rating sheets follow *Assignment 25.*

Assignment 24

Reading the longer poem aloud

AIM OF ASSIGNMENT: To refine your skills in projection of emotion through intensive rehearsal in reading selected emotional poetry aloud; to achieve listener appreciation; and to consider bodily action, voice control and rhythm in reading aloud.

LENGTH OF PERFORMANCE: Seven to ten minutes.

METHOD AND SUGGESTIONS: Again we call your attention to the basic skills of oral reading as you make your plans for this performance.

PROJECTS IN SPEAKING AND READING

Choice of material. Select a poem or poems that you like. You will profit most if you search for and select something which you have not read aloud before. It may be one long poem or several short ones. Check with your instructor to make sure that you have made a good selection.

Arrangement of material. Whether you choose to read a single long poem or several short ones, you will want to prepare some introductory remarks. These will probably include the titles, authors, background materials, and a word about your plan for the readings.

Projection of thought. First you must understand the thought content of the poem. This is sometimes difficult, because the form of poetry allows—often demands—that word order be inverted. You must know the meaning of each group of words that present a thought. Sometimes that includes less than a line; sometimes more. You should forget "line scheme," and "rhyme scheme."

Read the poem aloud to yourself quietly, searching for meaning. You may need to write a précis to come closer to understanding. Ask your instructor to hear you read it quietly. He will tell you if he understands the meaning as you read.

Projection of emotion. After you have the meaning mastered you are ready to search out "inner, deeper, richer meanings." Identify the emotions of each phrase.

Practice easily and quietly at first. Then as you begin to feel the emotion of the parts of the poem, let out a little. Use more vocal response and bodily action. Put more energy and vitality into the reading. Keep going until you have as much as the poem seems to call for, and as much as your audience is likely to accept in the circumstances of the reading—probably your classroom at the class hour.

Control of bodily activity. Remember that you are reading from the printed page. This means that you should stand still. Do not do much acting—not much bodily action, aside from facial gestures plus some shoulder, arm and hand movement.

If your book is on a reading stand, keep one hand on the page, with your finger on the place, so that when you look back at the text you will find the place quickly. If you hold the book in your hand do not wave it around. Hold it still. At times it is good to put your free hand on the page. Gesture very little.

Rhythm. Here you have a problem. For too long we have heard children "recite" poems in a sing-song manner dictated by the line and rhyme of the writing. You must break this down, unless the poem was written with the intention that it should be "sung." Some things of Vachel Lindsay, for example, depend on the rhythm for their effect. Most poetry, however, was written for meaning, and for that reason you should read for meaning, and let the emotion come out of the meaning, rather than from the form of the writing.

Again, use variety in pausing, speeding up, and slowing down. Ask your instructor to hear you with the purpose of suggesting variety in rhythm. Again, practice with a tape recorder. Consciously try for rhythm changes. Finally, after much practice, use only those rhythm variations that you believe the audience will accept and respond to.

Pronunciation. The first consideration is whether the poem is reflective of the speech of a region, or of a dialect of some English speaking group. If there are regional idiosyncrasies or dialect, find out how to do that type of pronunciation. It may be that no one can help you. In that case, discard that material—or, go ahead and try it, doing the best you can, remembering one thing: your audience must understand what you say, even in dialect.

If there is no specific call for an unusual pronunciation, then be sure you *know how* to pronounce each word the poet has written—and pronounce them that way.

Voice control. You may enjoy a lot of intensive work here. Mood, feelings, emotion are best projected through voice quality. Rate, intensity, and pitch are only slightly less important.

Analyze the printed poem, and mark it, thought group by thought group, with symbols of your own designing to identify the emotion. Practice each portion aloud, with and without a tape recorder. Then work on the complete selection, trying to get the emotional content of the pages into your voice.

Audience response. Your audience will respond best to a total unified effort on your part. Outside influences, such as the temperature of the room, the time of day, the imminence of the class-hour bell will also work upon them. Do your best to prepare the poem for their response to be what you want it. You must get their interest at once, hold it, and stir them to an appreciation of both the thought content of the poem and its emotional impact.

Assignment 25

The eulogy

Today, more and more people have the chance to read a speech they have written themselves. This is particularly true of people who appear on television. Many people speaking in public wish to be very careful to say exactly what they mean. For an assignment in this course, the eulogy may serve very well. It has before. Perhaps your instructor will substitute another type of speech to write out in full.

AIM OF ASSIGNMENT: To provide practice in writing a speech, with emphasis on choice of language and speech composition; and to provide further opportunity to rehearse carefully for the purpose of reading aloud from the printed page.

LENGTH OF PERFORMANCE: Seven to ten minutes.

METHOD AND SUGGESTIONS: Follow the basic skills for speech composition and reading aloud. Your performance will be enjoyed by your audience mainly as an oral reading.

Choice of subject. The eulogy is a speech in praise of the accomplishments or personal characteristics of some person no longer living. For this assignment, we ask that you select as the one you plan to praise, someone you have known personally, or someone among your own ancestors. This means that many of you will pick a grandfather or grandmother, an uncle or aunt, perhaps a parent or a brother or sister. By doing this you will have the most real speaking situation of the course. It goes far beyond the usual classroom assignment, because you are so closely concerned. In some families there are members of earlier generations who are still talked about with praise by the present members. You may wish to talk about that person. Or it may be that in your home town there was a person whom you knew, and about whom you would like to write and deliver a eulogy.

Choice of thought. You need a central thought. It is successfully stated as: "My grandfather lived by a simple rule of life," or "My aunt had traits of character that made her beloved by all who knew her," or "We remember our small cousin for her sweet disposition." You will think of the specific central idea that applies to the person you are eulogizing. Then you must decide on the subpoints. These will often be incidents from your subject's life that illustrate your central thought.

Choice of material and organization of material. Somewhere in the course of the speech, perhaps early, you will need to give certain facts about the life of your individual—his birth, education, occupation, achievements, and death. From then on you may spend your time presenting instances from his life that illustrate the central thought and main subpoints.

When your preparation has reached this point, get it down on paper, in outline form. Show it to your instructor for his criticism.

Use of language. You now are ready to do some writing. This is where the difficulty comes. You will be tempted to write an essay. But if you were to try to present a talk from your outline notes—and if you should record that speech on a tape recorder, you would find that you do not speak like an essay. Spoken sentences are shorter than written sentences. Words are simpler. There are times when you speak fragmentary groups of words, incomplete sentences. Your oral composition has informalities about it—contractions, and personal pronouns—that you don't use in an essay.

If you do not have a tape recorder on which you can tape your speech, and from which you can later transcribe it, then try this: speak through the talk once, all the way. This will put it briefly in mind. Then say it aloud again. Go very slowly trying as you do, to write fast enough to get down what you said. Use any kind of short hand or speed writing that you can.

Now, write or type this first draft. Show it to your instructor for criticism of organization and choice of material and thought.

Next, work over the composition, smoothing out grammatical inaccuracies. Check for unnecessary repetitions. Work over your use of words. You want it to sound like you, talking, but you should want it to sound like you at your sincere, cultured best. Write out this second draft. Submit it for evaluation of your use of words.

Let the third draft be prepared for the speaker's stand. Ask yourself some questions as you are doing this preparation: Have I said exactly what I want to say? Are my words, phrases, and sentences specific? Am I using varied language? Does it sound like me talking? Are my sentences too long or too short? Is there variety in the composition? And finally, check to see that you have given dignity and beauty to your use of language.

Projection to the audience. You will find that you are sincere. You are talking about someone near to you. You may wish to be more reserved and quiet for this speech than for some others you have made.

Projection of thought. The thoughts are your own. The writing is your own. Projection of thought will not give you difficulty.

Projection of emotion. There will be emotional content in this talk. The audience will realize the closeness of the person to you. You will not have difficulty. And if you have rehearsed the presentation enough times you will not be surprised by the sound of your voice in an emotional passage. For some this is a disturbing experience. They are actually living the emotion at the moment. Be sure to rehearse it many times.

Control of bodily activity. Use a well-lighted reading stand for the speech. Practice with your manuscript. Have a typed paper, double or triple spaced. Learn to slide the pages to the side rather than turn them over.

Limit your bodily action. Stand still. You probably will not need gestures. Your face will reflect your thinking well enough. You need not practice facial expressions for this speech. Practice looking up as though at the audience as you read.

Rhythm. This will be controlled by your thought and feeling during the reading. The important thing is that the speech should sound like you when you talk. If you have read it aloud frequently when you were writing it, you probably have a fine rhythm established.

PROJECTS IN SPEAKING AND READING

Pronunciation. Be correct, accurate, clear, and dignified.

Voice control. You probably will naturally keep the pitch of your voice low. Read easily and quietly. Use a narrow range of intensity. Just be sure that those in the rear are able to hear. They will give you their best attention, so you will be heard.

Audience response. They will be absorbed in the person you are eulogizing. Be sure that everything you do blends into a unified, total effect of dignified encomium.

ACHIEVEMENT IN READING ALOUD

Assignment No. _____   Student _____

Date _____   Selection _____   Author _____

Comments:

Choice of Material	7	6	5	4	3	2	1
Arrangement of Material	7	6	5	4	3	2	1
Projection of Thought	7	6	5	4	3	2	1
Projection of Emotion	7	6	5	4	3	2	1
Control of Bodily Activity	7	6	5	4	3	2	1
Rhythm	7	6	5	4	3	2	1
Pronunciation	7	6	5	4	3	2	1
Voice Control	7	6	5	4	3	2	1
Audience Response	7	6	5	4	3	2	1

Total score _____

7—Superior
6—Very Good
5—Good
4—Adequate
3—Poor
2—Very Poor
1—Inferior

Distribution

Above 49—Excellent
41 to 49—Good
32 to 40—Average
Below 32—Poor

Evaluator _____

PROJECTS IN SPEAKING AND READING

ACHIEVEMENT IN READING ALOUD

Assignment No. _____   Author _____

Date _____   Selection _____   Student _____

Comments:

Choice of Material	7	6	5	4	3	2	1
Arrangement of Material	7	6	5	4	3	2	1
Projection of Thought	7	6	5	4	3	2	1
Projection of Emotion	7	6	5	4	3	2	1
Control of Bodily Activity	7	6	5	4	3	2	1
Rhythm	7	6	5	4	3	2	1
Pronunciation	7	6	5	4	3	2	1
Voice Control	7	6	5	4	3	2	1
Audience Response	7	6	5	4	3	2	1

Total score _____

7—Superior
6—Very Good
5—Good
4—Adequate
3—Poor
2—Very Poor
1—Inferior

Distribution

Above 49—Excellent
41 to 49—Good
32 to 40—Average
Below 32—Poor

Evaluator _____

ACHIEVEMENT IN READING ALOUD

Assignment No. _____   Author _____

Date _____   Selection _____   Student _____

Comments:

Choice of Material	7	6	5	4	3	2	1
Arrangement of Material	7	6	5	4	3	2	1
Projection of Thought	7	6	5	4	3	2	1
Projection of Emotion	7	6	5	4	3	2	1
Control of Bodily Activity	7	6	5	4	3	2	1
Rhythm	7	6	5	4	3	2	1
Pronunciation	7	6	5	4	3	2	1
Voice Control	7	6	5	4	3	2	1
Audience Response	7	6	5	4	3	2	1

Total score _____

7—Superior
6—Very Good
5—Good
4—Adequate
3—Poor
2—Very Poor
1—Inferior

Distribution

Above 49—Excellent
41 to 49—Good
32 to 40—Average
Below 32—Poor

Evaluator _____

Appendix

34   Vocabulary development

Here is a list of many frequently used words. From time to time, write a sentence using one. Then find directly related words in a thesaurus or a dictionary of synonyms. Rewrite the sentence, retaining the intention of the original, but shading the meaning with a related word.

As you prepare a speech, check over this list. Select several that you are confident that you will use. Search out different words that mean very much the same. Plan to use one of them in your speech, replacing the word you would have used, but which has assumed a dullness and triteness through overuse.

able	always	bank	but	complete
above	amount	because	buy	connection
accept	answer	before	by	contract
account	any	beg	care	copy
address	appreciate	being	change	cost
advise	as	believe	charge	country
after	ask	better	check	course
again	at	between	class	cover
ago	attention	big	close	cut
all	back	bring	cold	dear
almost	bad	business	come	delay
also	balance	busy	company	desire

doubt	hope	new	reference	supply
during	house	next	regard	suppose
early	however	nice	regret	sure
end	if	note	remain	tell
enough	in	number	remember	that
even	interest	office	reply	then
except	just	old	report	therefore
expect	keep	opportunity	rest	think
express	kind	open	right	thought
far	large	order	room	too
favor	last	over	run	trouble
first	leave	own	same	trust
following	less	paper	satisfactory	take
for	life	part	second	talk
forward	like	party	see	try
found	list	pay	seem	unable
friend	little	people	service	under
furnish	long	place	set	upon
further	look	play	several	use
general	lot	please	short	value
give	love	pleasure	show	want
glad	make	position	since	war
go	many	possible	small	waste
good	man	present	some	way
great	meet	price	soon	which
guess	mind	prompt	sorry	who
hand	money	question	special	whole
happy	much	read	state	wish
hard	must	ready	statement	with
hear	name	real	stay	work
help	near	reason	still	world
high	necessary	receive	stock	yet
home	need	recent	subject	young

35   Articulation drills

Everyone profits from articulation drills at some time in his speech training. At the outset, try articulating all the words in the following lists. Then limit your practice to those which are of most value to you. When your instructor makes an inventory of your speech habits, he probably will check certain sounds that are faulty. Practice them, using these lists.

The organization of these words is done on two bases: first they are grouped according to a sound commonly misarticulated, such as

[s] [z] [θ] and [ð]. Within these groups there are three subdivisions, in most cases. The first presents words wherein the sound comes in the initial position, at the beginning of the word. Next, are those words in which the sound is in a medial position. And third, you will find the sound in the terminal position.

[s]
said
sake
sample
sea
serve
set
sick
site
social
soil
solid
some
soon
south
sum
supreme
sustain

absorb
agency
aside
baseball
closely
concede
deceit
erased
gossip
himself
innocent
loosed
myself
person
receipt
specific
wrestler

across
advance
base
bonus
coarse

confess
dangerous
decrease
doubtless
exerts
goose
intense
nice
produce
types
voice
yes

[z]
zany
zeal
zebra
zenith
zephyr
zero
zest
zinc
zinnia
zipper
zircon
zodiac
zone
zoo
Zulu

bazaar
busy
chosen
crazy
desire
easily
magazine
pleasant
prison
praised
result
spasm

stanza
thousand
used
visible
visor

amuse
because
birds
bonds
browse
cabins
chose
clubs
colors
girls
hands
miles
refuse
these
those
was
whose

[ʍ]
whack
whaler
wharf
whatever
wheelbarrow
whenever
whereabouts
whereby
wherefore
wherein
whereof
whereon
wherever
which
while
whimper
whine

whinny
whirlpool
whisk
whither

anywhere
awhile
everywhere
bewhiskered
everywhere
nowhere
somewhat
somewhere

[w]
wage
wait
wake
wall
war
wash
waste
water
we
wear
week
weight
well
were
wife
will
wind
winter
wisdom
woman
wonder
world

away
awoke
beware
bewitch

downward
glassware
lengthwise
midwinter
Milwaukee
outwit
rewind
seaweed
Southwest
tradewinds
twelve
twenty
twist
underworld
unwelcome
unwise
upward

[θ]
thank
theatre
theme
theory
thick
thief
third
thirty
thought
thousand
three
thread
thrift
through
throw

anything
Arthur
authority
Bertha
faithful
Gotham
healthy

140

APPENDIX

marathon	mother	issue	occasion	matches
method	neither	machinery	persuasion	merchants
nothing	northern	official	pleasure	orchard
northwest	rhythm	published	precision	parched
one-third	southern	rushing	provision	purchases
sympathy	together	session	regime	reaches
toothache	within	suspicious	seclusion	richest
twenty-three	worthy	threshed	seizure	teaching
wealthy			transfusion	touched
worthless	bathe	cash	treasure	watching
	breathe	crash	version	
breath	clothe	dish	vision	branch
both	lathe	distinguish		catch
death	lithe	English	barrage	clinch
earth	loathe	finish	beige	coach
faith	scathe	fish	camouflage	crutch
forth	seethe	flourish	concierge	detach
growth	smooth	foolish	corsage	etch
length	soothe	harsh	cortege	each
month	teethe	Irish	garage	much
mouth	tithe	marsh	massage	peach
north	with	rash	menage	pitch
south	writhe	refresh	mirage	porch
seventh		rush	prestige	rich
strength	[ʃ]	smash	rouge	search
teeth	Chicago	wash	sabotage	such
tooth	shade			trench
youth	shall	[ʒ]	[tʃ]	which
	shape	azure	chain	
[ð]	she	casual	chair	[dʒ]
than	sheep	casualty	chamber	gem
that	shelf	collusion	chapter	general
the	ship	composure	charm	gypsy
their	shirk	conclusion	chase	Japan
them	shoot	confusion	check	jam
then	shop	conversion	chew	jaw
there	short	decision	chick	jerk
they	should	diversion	chief	jewel
this	shove	enclosure	child	jive
those	show	erosion	chill	join
though	shrug	evasion	chimney	judge
thus	sure	exclusion	chop	judicial
		excursion	chose	jump
although	ancient	explosion	chuck	junior
another	appreciate	exposure	churn	jury
brother	battleship	fusion		just
either	beneficial	inclusion	achieve	
father	bookshop	invasion	exchange	adjust
feather	direction	leisure	coaching	angel
further	education	measure	marching	budget

courageous
energy
engine
forger
gorgeous
injustice
intelligent
major
manager
object
original
religion
suggested
unjust

acreage
advantage
bridge
cottage
edge
exchange
indulge
knowledge
language
lodge
page
pledge
range
revenge
siege
storage
village

[t]
table
tall
task
ten
to
top
toward
trust
twirl

attack
bottom
captain
certain
debating
eighteen

Latin
return
until

bent
boat
bought
district
flat
important
not
rust
suggest

[d]
damp
day
deck
depend
discard
divide
dome
double
during

accident
bender
broadly
candy
editor
headline
ladies
modern
radio
sudden

ahead
arrested
complied
expected
ground
informed
period
spend
varied

[m]
make
may

me
member
merry
mild
monkey
move
my

amend
clamor
empire
example
foremost
homely
improve
primary
summary

aim
came
crime
germ
him
palm
roam
stem

[n]
knee
nation
near
neck
neighbor
never
new
next
night
not

annual
canoe
council
enough
envelope
final
funny
instance
leaned
many
minor

only
unable
unlike

again
began
Berlin
born
confine
even
green
lawn
million
ocean
opinion
position
sustain

[ŋ]
banks
congress
fingers
frank
gangster
Ingersoll
inked
length
Lexington
linger
Long Island
longer
lungs
mangle
rank
single
spangle
strength
sunk
Yankee

along
among
being
bring
carrying
causing
coming
cutting
eating
facing

hang
King
looking
losing
living
making
putting
ring
sang
slung
song
strong
sung
writing
young

[r]
rain
rapid
rate
read
remain
rest
rid
road
rock
rose
rub
ruin

area
arise
arrive
carbine
careen
every
garden
heroic
luxury
narrow
perhaps
prairie
purpose
surprise
terrify
very

are
before
buyer

care	appeal	gather	die	chow
cooler	awful	handicap	dry	cow
copper	battle	inhabit	fly	endow
ever	bell	ladder	fry	how
four	bottle	mathematics	high	now
her	brittle	natural	lie	plow
hour	cattle	package	my	prow
labor	cool	pant	pie	row
lower	dull	rang	ply	sow
paper	feel	rapid	pry	vow
pioneer	fuel	placid	rye	
poor	full	sample	sigh	
popular	hill	scratch	tie	[ɔɪ]
your	pool	task	try	oil
	school	travel		oilcloth
[l]	small	valley		ointment
lack	whole		[aʊ]	oyster
large		[aɪ]	ouch	
last	[æ]	aisle	ounce	appoint
laws	absence	eyes	ours	boil
lay	absolute	I	ourselves	coin
leave	accident	ice	outdoor	Detroit
leg	acid	icicle	outer	doily
life	add	ideal	outfield	embroider
like	admire	identical	outgrow	exploit
lip	affable	Idaho	outguess	foible
list	after	idle	outing	hoist
live	algebra	Iowa	outlaw	join
log	alkali	iron	outlet	joyous
lose	alley	island	outlook	loiter
lost	ambition	item	output	loyal
low	animal	ivy	outside	noise
lucky	answer	ivory	owl	poison
	apple			rejoice
alike	aptitude	admire	about	royal
allure	ashes	behind	accountant	soil
already	ask	climate	astounding	voice
believe	aspirin	diagonal	counted	void
below	atlas	diet	countess	
collar	atom	divine	county	ahoy
daily	avenue	entirely	doubtless	alloy
delicate	axis	fighter	down	annoy
fellow		likewise	endowment	boy
gallop	catch	pilot	house	convoy
Holland	crack	slightly	mountain	decoy
privilege	dance	wildly	sound	deploy
public	emphatic	writer	south	destroy
value	fact		towel	employ
valve	fast	buy	town	envoy
yellow	financial	cry		joy
			allow	
			brown	

APPENDIX

Roy	ermine	circuit	nerve	fir
toy	irk	concern	person	her
Troy	Irving	curve	search	inter
	urban	exert	shirt	occur
[ɝ] or [ɜ]	urbane	first	verse	purr
early	urge	flirt		refer
earliest	urn	further	cur	sir
earn		girl	defer	slur
earnest	assert	heard	deter	stir
earth	bird	learn	err	

Practice for accuracy

abolitionist	demonstrative	ignominiously	provocative
abstracted	denominational	imperceptibly	psychologically
accompaniment	descriptive	imperturbable	psychiatrist
adjective	deterioration	incomprehensible	pyramidal
administrative	determinedly	indistinguishable	quadruped
alphabetical	dilapidated	insinuation	querulous
amidst	dishonest	irregularity	radicalism
amongst	disobedient	journalistic	ragamuffin
arithmetic	distinguishable	justification	recapitulate
authenticity	dramatically	kindergarten	recrimination
bacterial	ecclesiastical	kitchenette	remunerative
bankruptcy	electromotive	laboratory	reprehensible
bashfulness	emancipation	legitimate	responsibility
beforehand	emphatically	likelihood	revolutionize
behavior	enigmatically	longitudinal	rigorously
beneficence	extraordinarily	luxuriant	ruminate
bibliography	familiarity	magnanimity	sanitarium
blessedness	figuratively	maladjustment	satisfactorily
boisterously	financially	manufacturer	scholasticism
bystander	flexibility	marmalade	scientifically
calamity	fraudulent	mobilization	sentimentalist
candidacy	generosity	modernistic	shipbuilding
capitalistic	genuineness	multitudinous	similitude
cannibalism	geographically	necessarily	solicitude
carelessly	gesticulating	nonconformist	spiritualism
characteristically	governmental	ornithologist	stalactite
chrysanthemum	grammatical	ostensibly	surreptitiously
civilization	gratuitous	paraphernalia	taskmaster
classification	guardianship	parliamentary	theologian
coincident	gymnasium	pathological	topographical
conciliatory	habiliment	perpendicular	triumphantly
conductivity	hallucination	pessimistic	unsophisticated
correspondingly	headquarters	philanthropic	utilitarian
dandelion	hippopotamus	physiognomy	vocabulary
decorative	homogeneous	potentiality	windshield
defenseless	hypothetical	premeditate	wretchedness
delightedly	identification	presumptuous	zoological

36   Pronunciation drills

Freshman speakers have mispronounced the following words. Have you? Do you?

During the course, pronounce each for some listener. Ask him to check those that you pronounced inaccurately. Check the pronunciations of these words. Learn to say them properly. Use them properly in your speeches.

about	aunt	bringing	closed	delightful
absence	auntie	broken	closing	delivered
accept	author	brothers	cloth	dentist
accident	automobile	brought	clothes	department
account	avenue	Buffalo	cloudy	depot
acquainted	average	build	coast	desert
acre	awfully	bureau	coats	deserve
acted	awhile	buried	collar	desk
addition	banquet	business	collected	Detroit
addresses	bargain	buying	colleges	didn't
adventure	bath	calf	comfort	dies
advise	battery	calling	common	different
affectionate	battle	calves	company	direction
afterwards	been	can't	concert	dirty
afternoon	became	capital	containing	dissappoint
against	because	captain	conversation	discovered
agriculture	beginning	cars	correct	disease
all right	being	case	costs	dishes
always	believe	catalog	costume	district
American	belongs	catch	cottage	divided
amusement	below	cattle	cotton	division
amusing	belt	caught	couldn't	dogs
angel	besides	cause	counting	don't
another	better	ceiling	county	doors
answer	between	certainly	cousin	double
anybody	beyond	certificate	covering	doubtful
apartment	biggest	chairs	cows	down
appreciate	bird	chances	creek	dozen
April	birthday	changes	crowded	drawing
arithmetic	booklet	cheerful	current	due
arrived	borrowed	Chicago	cute	duty
asked	bottle	chocolate	cutting	duties
athletics	bottom	Christmas	damage	dumb
attacked	bought	church	dances	easily
attendance	branches	Cincinnati	dangerous	Easter
attended	brass	cities	dearest	eating
auditorium	brick	climate	December	education

effort	fishing	haven't	loaded	opening
eggs	fitted	height	Los Angeles	operate
eighty	followed	history	luncheon	opinion
election	forest	holds	making	opposite
electric	foreign	hole	managers	ordering
elementary	forever	hospital	manners	organized
eleven	forget	hour	manual	ours
enclose	fortune	houses	manufacture	ourselves
engineer	forty	however	many	outside
English	forward	hundred	mass	packages
enjoying	fountain	hunting	material	painted
enter	friend	husband	matter	palace
entered	from	ice cream	meaning	parade
entertainment	funeral	idea	measure	paragraph
entrance	furniture	I'll	medicine	parcel
envelope	further	I'm	meeting	pardon
equipment	games	imagine	members	parties
escape	garage	immediately	mention	passed
especially	gasoline	important	metal	patience
et cetera	gather	including	mighty	patient
evenings	geography	increase	milk	pattern
everything	gentlemen	industry	Minneapolis	payments
example	get	instant	minutes	penmanship
excellent	gift	instead	mischief	perfectly
excepting	giving	institute	mischievous	perfumes
exchanging	glad	instrument	model	perhaps
excitement	glasses	interested	moment	perspiration
exercises	good-by	interesting	mostly	photograph
exhibit	going	invite	mountains	physical
expected	golden	isn't	mouth	piano
experience	good-night	January	must	picture
experiment	gotten	just	national	Pittsburgh
express	government	kept	natural	places
factories	grandfather	kindergarten	nearest	planted
fallen	grass	kindest	necessary	playing
families	greatest	kindle	needed	pleasant
farm	greetings	kindness	neglect	pleasure
farther	grievous	knew	nephew	pneumonia
favorite	grown	knowledge	new	poems
February	guilty	language	New Orleans	poor
feed	habits	larynx	newspaper	popular
fencing	half	laughing	New York	population
fifth	Halloween	learned	northern	position
figures	handkerchiefs	length	noted	possible
filed	handled	lesson	notice	posture
filling	hanging	liberty	occupied	potatoes
finally	hardest	library	officer	pouch
find	hardly	lining	often	pound
finished	hasn't	literature	oldest	powder
fished	hated	little	once	practice

president	ring	something	thrown	watched
pretend	roof	somewhere	tickled	water
pretty	room	south	tired	wedding
primary	route	spend	together	Wednesday
private	rural	spirit	tomorrow	western
probably	safest	stationery	tournament	what
problems	salary	stomach	treasure	whatever
produce	sample	student	treated	wheat
professor	San Francisco	studying	truly	wheel
program	satisfied	subjects	truth	whenever
property	Saturday	suddenly	Tuesday	where
quarrel	saying	suffering	twelfth	wherever
question	scheme	suggest	twentieth	whether
rabbits	schoolhouse	superintendent	twenty	which
railroad	science	support	typewriter	while
raising	Seattle	suppose	understanding	white
rather	secret	surprise	university	why
reached	secretary	sweater	unpleasant	with
realize	selected	sweetest	unusual	without
reason	sell	swimming	used	witness
recently	sends	system	usual	women
reception	separate	telegraph	valuable	wonderfully
refuse	settlement	terrible	victory	world
regular	several	text	village	wouldn't
remember	signature	Thanksgiving	violin	writer
represent	since	theatre	visited	yellow
requested	sixth	themselves	visitor	yesterday
resort	sixty	thirty	waited	your
respectfully	skating	thousand	wanting	you're
returning	snowing	thousands	wash	

37 Voice control

To have effective control of your voice means that you have command over the elements of voice: pitch, rate, volume, and quality. For most people, this control comes with much practice. We offer here a type of material that lends itself to practice in variety.

This is a child's story. If you read to the youngsters in your family you know that they are very severe critics. Once they have heard fine story tellers and readers on radio and television and at school and at library story hours, they insist that you too should read the characters with all the variety possible.

Try reading this story. It is not complete, but the portion we print provides opportunity to practice variety. Use your imagination. When Sojo talks, or when the animals talk, do your best to make them sound as a child would want them to sound.

This practice material is provided for your own use, not necessarily for classroom exercise. Practice it at home. Read it aloud to yourself, exaggerating almost wildly. Read it to youngsters in your family. With some success you may be encouraged to get the rest of the story, or other stories for children. It will serve you well, both in achieving variety in voice—thereby improving voice control—and perhaps in entertaining children.

SOJO

by Erick Berry

Sojo was a little boy who was always sleepy. He woke up sleepy in the morning. He yawned all day long. He dropped asleep over his lunch. He slept halfway through his dinner. And, if you'll ever believe it, he even went to sleep when he should have been working.

One morning his Mammy called him early to get up and go down to the pool and bring back water for the cabbages. That, if you haven't already guessed it, was on a Monday morning. Sojo rubbed his eyes and ate his breakfast and took a bowl and went down to the pool.

Pretty soon he lay down and began to finish his sleep. When he woke up he heard something sper-lashing and sper-loshing in the water. Sojo yawned and rubbed his eyes. And there, right spang in the middle of the pool was a quite small Elephant, a-squirting water over his back from a quite small trunk.

"It must be fun to do that," said Sojo, yawning politely behind his hand.

"Not very," said the quite small Elephant. "It's almost *too* easy." And he squirted a trunkful of water into the coconut trees.

"Look here," said Sojo, suddenly sitting up. "I know a place that would be just *loads* of fun to squirt water on. It's not far from here either."

"Is that so?" asked the quite small Elephant eagerly. "Where is this place?"

But Sojo shook his head sleepily. "You wouldn't really be inter-

148

ested," he decided after a moment. And he flopped back on the grass again and closed his eyes.

The quite small Elephant was silent for a time. Then he squirted another trunkful of water into the coconut trees.

Sojo opened one eye, ever so little.

The quite small Elephant came nearer.

"Hi," he said. "What would you take to show me this place? I'd like something more amusing to do. I've been doing this every single day for a whole week."

Sojo opened both eyes and sat up. "Oh, I wouldn't *take* anything for it. You're a friend of mine and I'd be glad to show you the place. It would be a sort of game. Mind you, it's a good game, but a sort of difficult one." He waited a moment, thinking. "No, I don't even know if you could play it."

"The game," he said, getting to his feet, "is to take a trunkful of water from here . . . and follow me."

With the quite small Elephant carrying his quite small trunk full of water Sojo went along the path to the garden where the cabbages grew.

"You see this is the game," explained Sojo. "You spray the water ver . . y carefully over the cabbages. If you spray it too hard and root up a cabbage you lose a point. And if you don't bring enough water and the cabbages dry up, you lose the game. But if you bring along four trunkfuls a morning every morning and make it a nice swimmy, sludgy marsh, you win the game. It's really a beautiful game."

"Oh, that does sound a beautiful game," said the quite small Elephant gratefully. "Like this?" And he sent out the water from his trunk in a long whish . . . who . . . o . . . osh all over the cabbages.

Sojo watched with his head on one side. "Not bad, for a first try. But you'll do a lot better with practice."

"Oh, yes indeed I shall," said the quite small Elephant anxiously. And he could. And he did.

Sojo leaned against a coconut tree and watched. And when the quite small Elephant had used up the fourth trunkful of water he woke up again.

"That was very good indeed," he said. "I think you won the game this morning. No doubt you'll do even better tomorrow."

"Please, can't I do it just once more?" said the quite small Elephant.

149

But Sojo shook his head. "Oh no. Four trys every morning is all you can have. Now come back tomorrow and see how much better you can do."

"Well, thank you tremendously," cried the quite small Elephant. And he trotted away.

And Sojo slid down to the foot of the shady coconut tree and went sound asleep. When his Mammy came to wake him she certainly was surprised to see how nicely the cabbages had been watered.

* * * * * * * * * *

Next morning Sojo's Mammy called him. "Get up and eat your breakfast," she said. "I want a garden dug, down beyond the cabbages. A new garden." And that, if you haven't already guessed it, was on a Wednesday morning.

Sojo rubbed his eyes and ate his breakfast. He took his hoe and went down beyond the cabbages to dig the new garden. He sat down under a coconut tree and looked at what he had to do. Pretty soon he rolled over and began to finish his sleep.

When he woke up he heard the funniest grunting and sk . . . uff . . .-ulufuling noise in the underbrush. So he yawned and sat up and straight ahead of him was a dark snout and two bright black eyes poking out through the brush. And then a quite small bristly black pig with two shiny white tusks followed the snout.

"Hi there, Pig!" said Sojo. And he got to his feet and began to dig busily with his hoe.

Pretty soon the quite small bristly black pig asked, "What are you doing, Sojo? Is it a game? Can't I play it too?"

Sojo shook his head and kept right on digging with his hoe. "It's just a silly game," he said. "You wouldn't be interested."

"How do you *know* I wouldn't be interested?" said the quite small pig crossly. "Just you let me try." And he started to shove Sojo away from the row he was hoeing.

But Sojo was firm. "No, it's a very difficult game and you have to play it just right. Now run along and don't bother me."

The quite small bristly black pig watched for a while longer. "What would you take to let me play that game too? I'll bet I'd be good at it."

Sojo stopped digging with his hoe. "I wouldn't *take* anything for it. You're a friend of mine, so I'll show you how, but I don't know if you could do it." So he did show him, and then he went and sat down under a tree.

The quite small black bristly pig began to dig with his tusks. He shoved and he pushed and he grunted and he scrabbled. And he went all the way down one row of the new garden. His two tusks were twice as sharp as Sojo's hoe, and much much faster. And he went down another row of the garden. And pretty soon he had finished it all.

And when Sojo woke up the quite small black bristly pig asked, "Now that's done what do I do next?"

"That's all there is," said Sojo. "But next time I play a nice game I'll let you know so you can come and play it too." And he went home, yawning, to his Mammy.

Sojo's Mammy certainly was surprised to see how nicely her new garden had been hoed.

* * * * * * * * * *

Next morning Sojo's Mammy called him to get up and go fishing. "Bring me a lot of fish for my dinner. Because I do like fish." And that, if you haven't already guessed it, was a Friday morning.

Sojo rubbed his eyes, and ate his breakfast. He took his fishing rods and his fishing lines and went down to the river. He stuck his fishing rods in the bank and put bait on his hooks, and threw the lines into the river.

Then he sat down under a tree and pretty soon he rolled over and began to finish his sleep.

When he woke up he saw a great huge bird a-sitting on a sandbar in the middle of the river catching fish. The great huge bird had a big fish-basket of skin right underneath his beak. And every time he caught a fish he'd pop it into the basket.

Sojo sat up and wriggled his fishlines. But there was nothing on any of them. Not one single solitary fish.

Then he yawned and called out to the great huge bird, "Hi, Pelican! Good fishing?"

"Excellent!" said the Pelican, tossing his fish into the air and catching it in his fish-basket beak. "Too good, in fact."

"How's that?" asked Sojo.

151

"Well, you see," said the Pelican, shifting his weight from one great flat foot to the other great flat foot on the sandbar, "I've eaten all I can hold, and my basket is full, and *still* I keep on catching fish. But if I put them back in the water they'll swim away and warn the other fish about me, and so tomorrow I won't be able to catch any."

Sojo thought for a few minutes, then he said, "You're a friend of mine, Pelican. Perhaps I can manage to help you out and take some of those fish off your hands. That is—off your beak. Just, of course, as a very special favor."

"Oh, would you?" said the Pelican, very pleased.

And he could. And he would. And he did. Sojo took two catfish and a dogfish, some mudfish and three eels. He put them all on a stick together and went home, yawning, to his Mammy.

And his Mammy certainly was surprised to see all the fine fish he had brought home. . . .

38   Spontaneous reading

The following selection is printed here to help you get a feeling for spontaneous reading. "Spontaneous" means doing it as you feel it, without former planning, as a result of impulse, without deliberation.

Try this passage many times. Just read it. Use it for class exercise. Use it at home when you have a few minutes extra, perhaps while you are rehearsing for another speech. Just read it aloud and enjoy it. Do whatever seems to be the thing to do at the time you are reading it.

The value of this exercise will come in your knowing that you can read aloud effectively. If you read in class, your audience will enjoy it. They will be pleased to hear you read this particular item. Do not try to analyze what you are doing. Do that with other material. Just read this spontaneously.

If you like the portion of the book printed here, get the rest of it. The story goes on to tell how Murchison tried to get rid of Fluff. Or try reading another of Ellis Parker Butler's stories, *Pigs Is Pigs*.

THAT PUP

by Ellis Parker Butler

Murchison, who lives next door to me, wants to get rid of a dog, and if you know of anyone who wants a dog I wish you would let Murchison know. Murchison doesn't need it. He is tired of dogs, anyway. That is just like Murchison. 'Way up in an enthusiasm one day and sick of it the next.

Brownlee—Brownlee lives on the other side of Murchison—remembers when Murchison got the dog. It was the queerest thing, so Murchison says, you ever heard of. Here came the express wagon— Adams' Express Company's wagon—and delivered the dog. The name was all right—"C. P. Murchison, Gallatin, Iowa"—and the charges were paid. The charges were $2.80, and paid, and the dog had been shipped from New York. Think of that! Twelve hundred miles in a box, with a can of condensed milk tied to the box and "Please feed" written on it.

When Murchison came home to dinner, there was the dog. At first Murchison was pleased; then he was surprised; then he was worried. He hadn't ordered a dog. The more he thought about it the more he worried.

"If I could just *think* who sent it," he said to Brownlee, "then I would know who sent it; but I can't think. It is evidently a valuable dog. I can see that. People don't send cheap, inferior dogs twelve hundred miles. But I can't *think* who sent it."

"What worries me," he said to Brownlee another time, "is who sent it. I can't *imagine* who would send me a dog from New York. I know so many people, and, like as not, some influential friend of mine has meant to make me a nice present, and now he is probably mad because I haven't acknowledged it. I'd like to know what he thinks of me about now!"

It almost worried him sick. Murchison never did care for dogs, but when a man is presented with a valuable dog, all the way from New York, with $2.80 charges paid, he simply *has* to admire that dog. So Murchison got into the habit of admiring the dog, and so did Mrs. Murchison. From what they tell me, it was rather a nice dog in its infancy, for it was only a pup then. Infant dogs have a habit of being pups.

As near as I could gather from what Murchison and Mrs. Murchison told me, it was a little, fluffy, yellow ball, with bright eyes and ever-moving tail. It was the kind of a dog that bounces around like a rubber ball, and eats the evening newspaper, and rolls down the porch steps with short, little squawks of surprise, and lies down on its back with its four legs in the air whenever a bigger dog comes near. In color it was something like a camel, but a little redder where the hair was long, and its hair was like beaver fur—soft and wooly inside, with a few long hairs that were not so soft. It was so little and fluffy that Mrs. Murchison called it Fluff. Pretty name for a soft, little dog is Fluff.

"If I only *knew* who sent that dog," Murchison used to say to Brownlee, "I would like to make some return. I'd send him a barrel of my best melons, express paid, if it cost me five dollars!"

Murchison was in the produce business, and he knew all about melons, but not so much about dogs. Of course he could tell a dog from a cat, and a few things of that sort, but Brownlee was the real dog man. Brownlee had two Irish pointers or setters—I forget which they were; the black dogs with the long, floppy ears. I don't know much about dogs myself. I hate dogs.

Brownlee knows a great deal about dogs. He isn't one of the book-taught sort; he knows dogs by instinct. As soon as he sees a dog he can make a guess at its breed ... Brownlee can look at any one of them and immediately guess at its formula—one part Spitz, three parts greyhound, two parts collie, and so on. I have heard him guess more kinds of dogs than I ever knew existed.

As soon as he saw Murchison's dog he guessed it was a pure bred Shepherd with a trace of Eskimo. Massett, who thinks he knows as much about dogs as Brownlee does, didn't believe it. The moment he saw the pup he said it was a pedigree dog, half St. Bernard and half Spitz.

Brownlee and Massett used to sit on Murchison's steps after supper and point out the proofs to each other. They would argue for hours.

"All right, Massett," Brownlee would say, "but you can't fool *me!* Look at that nose! If that isn't a Shepherd nose, I'll eat it. And see

154

that tail! Did you ever see a tail like that on a Spitz? That is an Eskimo tail as sure as I am a foot high."

"Tail fiddlesticks!" Massett would reply. "You can't tell anything by a pup's tail. Look at his ears! *There* is St. Bernard for you! And see his lower jaw. Isn't that Spitz? I'll leave it to Murchison. Isn't that lower jaw Spitz, Murchison?"

Then all three would take the puppy and open its mouth and feel its jaw, and the pup would wriggle and squeak, and back away, opening and shutting its mouth to see if its works had been damaged.

"All right!" Brownlee would say. "You wait a year or two and you'll see!"

About three months later the pup was as big as an ordinary full-grown dog, and his coat looked like a compromise between a calfskin and one of these hairbrush door mats you use to wipe your feet on in muddy weather. He did not look like the same pup. He was long limbed and awkward and useless, and homely as a shopworn fifty-cent yellow plush manicure set. Murchison began to feel that he didn't really need a dog, but Brownlee was as enthusiastic as ever. He would go over to Murchison's fairly oozing dog knowledge.

"I'll tell you what that dog is," he would say. "That dog is a cross between a Great Dane and an English Deerhound. You've got a very valuable dog there, Murchison, a very valuable dog. He comes of fine stock on both sides, and it is a cross you don't often see. I never saw it, and I've seen all kinds of crossed dogs."

Then Massett would drop in and walk around the dog admiringly for a few minutes and absorb his beauties.

"Murchison," he would say, "do you know what that dog is? That dog is a pure cross between a Siberian wolfhound and a Newfoundland. You treat that dog right and you'll have a fortune in him. Why, a pure Siberian wolfhound is worth a thousand dollars, and a good— a really good Newfoundland, mind you—is worth two thousand, and you've got both in one dog. That's three thousand dollars' worth of dog!"

In the next six months Fluff grew. He broadened out and lengthened and heightened, and every day or two Brownlee or Massett would discover a new strain of dog in him. They pointed out to Murchison all the marks by which he could tell the different kinds of dog that were combined in Fluff, and every time they discovered a

155

new one they held a sort of jubilee, and bragged and swelled their chests. They seemed to spend all their time thinking up odd and strange kinds of dog that Fluff had in him.

Murchison, not being a doggish man, never claimed to have noticed any of these family resemblances, and never said what he thought the dog really was until a month or two later, when he gave it as his opinion that the dog was a cross between a wolf, a Shetland pony, and hyena. It was about that time that Fluff had to be chained. He had begun to eat other dogs, and children and chickens. The first night Murchison chained him to his kennel Fluff walked half a mile, taking the kennel along, and then only stopped because the kennel got tangled with a lamp-post. The man who brought him home claimed that Fluff was nearly asphyxiated when he found him; said he gnawed half through the lamp-post, and that gas got in his lungs, but this was not true. Murchison learned afterwards that it was only a gasoline lamp-post, and a wooden one.

"If there were only some stags around this part of the country," said Massett, "the staghound strain in that dog would be mighty valuable. You could rent him out to everybody who wanted to go stag hunting; and you'd have a regular monopoly, because he's the only staghound in this part of the country. And stag hunting would be popular, too, out here, because there are no game laws that interfere with stag hunting in this State. There is no closed season. People could hunt stags all the year round, and you'd have that dog busy every day of the year."

"Yes!" sneered Brownlee, "only there are no stags. And he hasn't any staghound blood in him. Pity there are no Dachs in this State, too, isn't it? Then Murchison could hire his dog at night, too. They hunt Dachs at night, don't they, Massett? Only there is no Dachshund blood in him, either. If there *was*, and if there were a few Dachs—"

Massett was mad.

"Yes!" he cried. "And you, with your Cuban bloodhound strain! I suppose if it was the open season for Cubans, you'd go out with the dog and tree a few!"

Brownlee doesn't get mad easily.

"Murchison," he said, "leaving out Massett's dreary nonsense about staghounds, I can tell you that dog would make the finest duck dog

156

in the State. He's got all the points for a good duck dog, and I ought to know for I have two of the best duck dogs that ever lived. All he needs is training. If you will train him right you'll have a mighty valuable dog."

"But I don't hunt ducks," said Murchison, "and I don't know how to train even a lapdog."

"You let me attend to his education," said Brownlee. "I just want to show Massett here that I know a dog when I see one. I'll show Massett the finest duck dog he ever saw when I get through with Fluff."

So he went over and got his shotgun, just to give Fluff his first lesson. The first thing a duck dog must learn is not to be afraid of a gun, and Brownlee said that if a dog first learned about guns right at his home he was not so apt to be afraid of them. He said that if a dog heard a gun for the first time when he was away from home and in strange surroundings he was quite right to be surprised and startled, but if he heard it in the bosom of his family, with all his friends calmly seated about, he would think it was a natural thing, and accept it as such.

So Brownlee put a shell in his gun and Massett and Murchison sat on the porch steps and pretended to be uninterested and normal, and Brownlee stood up and aimed the gun in the air. Fluff was eating a bone, but Brownlee spoke to him and he looked up, and Brownlee pulled the trigger. It seemed about five minutes before Fluff struck the ground, he jumped so high when the gun was fired, and then he started north by northeast at about sixty miles an hour. He came back all right, three weeks later, but his tail was still between his legs.

Brownlee didn't feel the least discouraged. He said he saw now that the whole principle of what he had done was wrong; that no dog with any brains whatever could be anything but frightened to hear a gun shot off right in the bosom of his family. That was no place to fire a gun. He said Fluff evidently thought the whole lot of us were crazy, and ran in fear of his life, thinking we were insane and might shoot him next. He said the thing to do was to take the shotgun into its natural surroundings and let Fluff learn to love it there. He pictured Fluff enjoying the sound of the gun when he heard it at the edge of the lake.

Murchison never hunted ducks, but as Fluff was his dog, he went with Brownlee, and of course Massett went. Massett wanted to see the failure. He said he wished stags were as plentiful as ducks, and he would show Brownlee!

Fluff was a strong dog—he seemed to have a strain of ox in him, so far as strength went—and as long as he saw the gun he insisted that he would stay at home; but when Brownlee wrapped the gun in brown paper so it looked like a big parcel from the meat shop, the horse that they had hitched to the buckboard was able to drag Fluff along without straining itself. Fluff was fastened to the rear axle with a chain.

When they reached Duck Lake, Brownlee untied Fluff and patted him, and then unwrapped the gun. Fluff gave one pained glance and made the six-mile run home in seven minutes without stopping. He was home before Brownlee could think of anything to say, and he went so far into his kennel that Murchison had to take off the boards at the back to find him that night.

"That's nothing," was what Brownlee said when he did speak; "young dogs are often that way. Gun fright. They have to be gun broken. You come out to-morrow, and I'll show you how a man who really knows how to handle a dog does the trick."

The next day, when Fluff saw the buckboard he went into his kennel, and they couldn't pry him out with the hoe-handle. He connected buckboards and guns in his mind, so Brownlee borrowed the butcher's delivery wagon, and they drove to Wild Lake. It was seven miles, but Fluff seemed more willing to go in that direction than toward Duck Lake. He did not seem to care to go to Duck Lake at all.

"Now, then," said Brownlee, "I'll show you the intelligent way to handle a dog. I'll prove to him that he has nothing to fear, that I am his comrade and friend. And at the same time," he said, "I'll not have him running off home and spoiling our day's sport."

So he took the chain and fastened it around his waist, and then sat down and talked to Fluff like an old friend, and got him in a playful mood. Then he had Murchison get the gun out of the wagon and lay it on the ground about twenty feet off. It was wrapped in brown paper.

Brownlee talked to Fluff and told him what fine sport duck hunting is, and then, as if by chance, he got on his hands and knees and crawled toward the gun. Fluff hung back a little, but the chain just

158

coaxed him a little, too, and they edged up to the gun, and Brownlee pretended to discover it unexpectedly.

"Well, well!" he said. "What's this?"

Fluff nosed up to it and sniffed it, and then went at it as if it was Massett's cat. That Brownlee had wrapped a beefsteak around the gun, inside the paper, and Fluff tore off the paper and ate the steak, and Brownlee winked at Murchison.

"I declare," he said, "if here isn't a gun! Look at this, Fluff—a gun! Gosh! but we are in luck!"

Would you believe it, that dog sniffed at the gun, and did not fear it in the least? You could have hit him on the head with it and he would not have minded it. He never did mind being hit with small things like guns and ax handles.

Brownlee got up and stood erect.

"You see!" he said proudly. "All a man needs with a dog like this is intelligence. A dog is like a horse. He wants his reason appealed to. Now, if I fire the gun, he may be a little startled, but I have created a faith in me in him. He knows there is nothing dangerous in a gun *as* a gun. He knows I am not afraid of it, so he is not afraid. He realizes that we are chained together, and that proves to him that he need not run unless I run. Now watch."

Brownlee fired the shotgun.

Instantly he started for home. He did not start lazily, like a boy starting to the wood pile, but went promptly and with a dash. His first jump was only ten feet, and we heard him grunt as he landed, but after that he got into his stride and made fourteen feet each jump. He was bent forward a good deal in the middle, where the chain was, and in many ways he was not as graceful as a professional cinder-path track runner, but, in running, the main thing is to cover the ground rapidly. Brownlee did that.

Massett said it was a bad start. He said it was all right to start a hundred-yard dash that way, but for a long-distance run—a run of seven miles across country—the start was too impetuous; that it showed a lack of generalship, and that when it came to the finish the affair would be tame; but it wasn't.

Brownlee said afterwards that there wasn't a tame moment in the entire seven miles. It was rather more wild than tame. He felt right from the start that the finish would be sensational, unless the chain cut him quite in two, and it didn't. He said that when the chain had cut as far as his spinal column it could go no farther, and it stopped and clung there, but it was the only thing that did stop, except his breath. It was several years later that I first met Brownlee, and he was still breathing hard, like a man who has just been running rapidly. Brownlee says when he shuts his eyes his legs still seem to be going.

The first mile was through underbrush, and that was lucky, for the underbrush removed most of Brownlee's clothing, and put him in better running weight, but at the mile and a quarter they struck the road. He said at two miles he thought he might be overexercising the dog and maybe he had better stop, but the dog seemed anxious to get home so he didn't stop there. He said that at three miles he was sure the dog was overdoing, and that with his knowledge of dogs he was perfectly able to stop a running dog in its own length if he could speak to it, but he couldn't speak to this dog for two reasons. One was that he couldn't overtake the dog and the other was that all the speak was yanked out of him.

When they reached five miles the dog seemed to think they were taking too much time to get home, and let out a few more laps of speed, and it was right there that Brownlee decided that Fluff had some greyhound blood in him.

He said that when they reached town he felt as if he would have been glad to stop at his own house and lie down for awhile, but the dog didn't want to, and so they went on; but that he ought to be thankful that the dog was willing to stop at that town at all. The next town was twelve miles farther on, and the roads were bad. But the dog turned into Murchison's yard and went right into his kennel.

When Murchison and Massett got home, an hour or so later, after driving the horse all the way at a gallop, they found old Gregg, the carpenter, prying the roof off the kennel. You see, Murchison had knocked the rear out of the kennel the day before, and so when the dog aimed for the front he went straight through, and as Brownlee was built more perpendicular than the dog, Brownlee didn't go quite through. He went in something like doubling up a dollar bill to put it into a thimble. I don't suppose anyone would *want* to double up a dollar bill to put it into a thimble, but neither did Brownlee want to be doubled up and put into the kennel. It was the dog's thought. So they had to take the kennel roof off.

When they got Brownlee out they laid him on the grass, and covered him up with a porch rug, and let him lie there a couple of hours to pant, for that seemed what he wanted to do just then. It was the longest period Brownlee ever spent awake without talking about dog.

Murchison and Massett and old Gregg and twenty-six informal guests stood around and gazed at Brownlee panting. Presently Brownlee was able to gasp out a few words.

"Murchison," he gasped, "Murchison, if you just had that dog in Florence—or wherever it is they race dogs—you'd have a fortune."

He panted awhile, and then gasped out:

"He's a great runner; a phenomenal runner!"

He had to pant more, and then he gasped with pride:

"But I wasn't three feet behind him all the way!"